Learn, Lead and Leave a Legacy: *Advancing Women to the Top*

Complied by:
LaKisha C. Brooks, M.S., M.Ed.

With contributing authors:

Sabrina Brawner, Latasha Kinnard and Aisha Martin

Copyright © 2015 Brooks Enterprise and Consultants

All rights reserved.

ISBN-13: 978-1515113782

ISBN-10: 1515113787

Cover Design: StarChild Graphics

Editor: LaKisha C. Brooks, MS, M.Ed.

Co-editor: Sabrina Brawner

Table of Contents

Author's Bio..iv

Introduction..vi

Chapter 1 The Why, What and How to Advance Women in the Workplace?...7

Chapter 2 Unequal Pay in the Workplace and the Consequences for Women and Society..22

Chapter 3 Demanding and Earning Respect in the Workplace..........35

Chapter 4 Work-Life Balance...55

Chapter 5 "Standitioning" from the Workplace to Entrepreneurship.70

Conclusion..80

References..83

Author's Bio

LaKisha C. Brooks, M.S., M.Ed, an internationally recognized women's leadership expert, has been featured on ABC, FOX, CW, and NBC affiliates across the country, as well as, The Denver Post and The Miami Herald. She is a firm believer that "everyone has the ability to be a great leader" and has conducted research on the need for leadership development for college students. She has a Bachelor's degree in Speech Communications from Georgia State University and two Master's degrees, one in Administrative Leadership and a second in Training and Development from Central Michigan University. LaKisha's big break came when she was cast as a mentor/ life coach on MTV's hit show MADE. LaKisha is a trailblazer in women's leadership and empowerment and lives by the motto of "Create the Strength, Discipline and Freedom to Define Your Self". She is also the author of the book, *Leadership's Got Everything to Do With It! Women's Guide to the Sustainable Leader and Organization*.

As the former Ms. Alabama US, LaKisha travels the country promoting her platform, "Learn, Lead and Leave a Legacy in the Workplace", challenging women through leadership. She also works as a career, life and leadership coach focusing on the areas of resume writing, interviewing, communication, leadership development and job search strategies, conflict management, teambuilding, emotional intelligence and goal setting. Moreover, she performs speeches and hosts workshops on these and other topics and has worked with organizations and groups such as Clark Atlanta University, Georgia State University, Girls Inc. Atlanta Children's Shelter, The Professional Women's Group and more. In 2012, Lakisha awarded five high school senior and junior girls with leadership and community service awards, makeovers and prom dresses at the "Model Within Me" Award show ceremony. In October 2014, LaKisha created the Women of Excellence in Leadership Award Show (WELA) for eight talented women in the Metro Atlanta area for their excellence in leadership. Some people are born leaders and spend their lives striving to empower us as well; Lakisha is one of those individuals. Those who she touches have their lives enriched just by virtue of the encounter.

Introduction

In 2008, the United States made history by electing its first African American president. 2016 may find the country again making history, as former Secretary of State and Democratic presidential candidate Hillary Clinton is vying to become the country's first female president. Though the notion of a female president is gratifying for many women and feminists alike, it would only serve as a consolation prize, as woman are still facing issues in today's job market. Women are challenging the status quo in the United States. They are fighting to see a shift in leadership in the workplace and will not stop fighting until this change occurs.

From the perceptive of four female millennials, this compilation book covers prevalent issues plaguing women in the United States' workforce. Such issues include a lack of female representation in leadership and decision making positions, unequal pay, disrespect in the workplace, and inadequate work-life balance. After completing this book, readers will gain insight to remedies that will alleviate ongoing problems hindering women in the workplace.

Chapter 1

The What, Why and How to Advance Women in the Workplace

By: LaKisha C. Brooks, MS, M.Ed.
CEO, Brooks Enterprise and Consultants
Women's Leadership Expert
Founder, Women of Excellence in Leadership Awards
Award Winning Speaker

History of Women Equality in the Workplace and Society

The 1960s found more women yearning for more opportunities outside the home. They relished in the notion of having a career, becoming an entrepreneur, opening a bank account or simply having a "voice". This is because prior to the 1960's women's revolution, women's roles were limited to being subservient to their husbands, bearing children, and other domestic duties. Even television shows in that era, such as *Leave It To Beaver* [1] and *Bewitched* [2], mirrored the reality for most women, portraying them as nothing more than uneducated housewives.

In 1963, Betty Friedan penned the *Feminine Mystic* [3], a revolutionary piece of literature that surveyed the lives of housewives during that period. Additionally, the book gave light to the real frustrations of women and "defined the silent struggle women faced: they were unhappy in their domestic roles, but society insisted that being a housewife was the best way to find fulfillment" [4].

---

[1] Connelly, J., Moshe, B. (1957). "Leave It Beaver". Los Angeles, CA: Columbia Broadcasting System and American Broadcasting Company
[2] Ackerman, H. (1964). "Bewitched". Los Angeles, CA: American Broadcasting Company
[3] Friedan, B. (1963). *Feminine Mystique*. New York, NY
[4] Meyers, L. (2013). Peek Inside the Book That Sparked a Second Wave of Feminism. Retrieved from: http://www.popsugar.com/love/Betty-Friedan-Feminine-Mystique-Quotes-28158627

In addition to her book, Friedan became the first president of the National Organization for Women (NOW), an organization founded in 1966 by Friedan and 27 other individuals. The purpose of the organization "is to take action to bring women into full participation in the mainstream of American society now, exercising all privileges and responsibilities thereof in truly equal partnership of men"[5]

Not only were there a number of organizations and movements, such as the Civil Rights Act of 1964, changing how women were viewed in the household and the workplace, but entertainment and television was changing as well. Marlo Thomas', *That Girl*[6] in 1966, was one the first shows that portrayed a single working woman on television. In 1968, *Julia*[7], starring Diahann Carroll, not only depicted an African American woman in a different light, but also chronicled the life of a widowed, working mother. The 1960's also found women slowly obtaining jobs, starting businesses, opening bank accounts and searching for financial freedom.

In 1972, the face of the Chief Executive Officer (CEO) in corporate America began to change as Katherine Graham became the first female CEO of a Fortune 500 Company. Since then, women have made strides in closing the gender gap for leadership and decision making roles in the United States, but there is still work to be done. Moreover, according to Catalyst, there are only 23 female CEOs of Fortune 500 companies; that is a dismal 4.6%.[8]

This chapter will examine why women should be in leadership positions, discuss how women, companies and the government play a role in advancing women and offer solutions to alleviate the problem.

---

[5] When and how was NOW founded? (n.d.). Retrieved on March 22, 2015 from: http://now.org/faq/when-and-how-was-now-founded/
[6] Sam Denoff, S., Persky, B., Thomas, M., Thomas, D. (1966). "That Girl". Los Angeles, CA: American Broadcasting Company
[7] Kante, H. (1968). "Julia". Los Angeles, CA: American Broadcasting Company
[8] Women CEOs of the S&P 500. (2015) Catalyst. Retrieved on April 6, 2015 from: http://www.catalyst.org/knowledge/women-ceos-sp-500

The What, Why and How to Advancing Women in the Workplace

There is still a lack of women in leadership roles, and without a concrete plan of attack, this situation may not change. Before a plan can be devised, the problem must first be properly diagnosed. Furthermore, we should determine why this situation should be remedied and evaluate what affect it has on our society, our economy and the future.

What is the problem?

The first step in combating this problem is to determine there is actually a problem.

Women are not Advancing as Quickly as Men

According to a study, women obtain 53% of entry level positions.[9] Despite that, women are still not advancing as quickly as men. Unfortunately, only 35 percent of women who start in entry level positions go on to director level, 24 percent to the senior vice president level and 19 percent to the C- level.[10]

Wage Gap

There is a gender wage gap in the United States. On average, women are making 78 cents to the dollar compared to white men doing the exact same job. For some races, such as Hispanic and Black, that gap is even greater, 56 cents for Hispanic women and 64 cents for Black women, for every dollar earned by white men.[11]

---

[9] Shellenberger, S. (2012) The XX Factor: What's Holding Women Back? The Wall Street Journal. Retrieved on June 1, 2014 from: http://online.wsj.com/news/articles/SB10001424052702304746604577381953238775784
[10] Ibid
[11] O'Brien, S. A.(n.d.). 78 cents on the dollar: The facts about the gender wage gap. CNN Money. Retrieved from: http://money.cnn.com/2015/04/13/news/economy/equal-pay-day-2015/

Limited Number of Women on Boards

There is a limited amount of women serving on the board for Fortune 500 companies. In 2013, 50 of the Fortune 500 companies had no female directors. [12]

Identifying the problem is just the first step in changing the face of leadership in the United States. We must now determine why women are needed in leadership and decision making roles, as well as examine factors that are holding women back from advancing.

Why is it Important to Have Women in Leadership and Decision Making Roles?

Increase a Company's Bottom Line

Women are an important and essential part of the United States' economy. Women have immense purchasing power and, in most cases, are the primary decision makers when making purchasing decisions in most households. So would it not be logical to put women in leadership positions as they would know how to market and relate to women who are primary purchasers?

In addition, a Gallup article written by Sangeeta Bharadwaj Badal, states "gender-diverse business units in the retail company have 14% higher average comparable revenue than less-diverse business units and gender-diverse business units in the hospitality company show 19% higher average quarterly net profit ($16,296 vs. $13,702) than less-diverse business units."[13]

---

[12] Fairchild, C.(2015). The 23 Fortune 500 companies with all-male boards. Fortune Magazine. Retrieved on March 2, 2015 from: http://fortune.com/2015/01/16/fortune-500-companies-with-all-male-boards/

[13] Badal, S. B. (2014). The Business Benefits of Gender Diversity.Gallup. Retrieved on March 16, 2015 from: http://www.gallup.com/businessjournal/166220/business-benefits-gender-diversity.aspx

These figures are just a few indicators that illustrate the significance of considering women in leadership roles when evaluating a company's bottom line.

Different Perspective

As previously mentioned, women are primary decision makers in their households. This can come as an advantage when marketing and selling products, services and goods. With women at the helm, companies are able to plan and implement strategies from a woman's perspective. This perspective can also lead to creativity and innovation. A company may have previously overlooked this because they continue the same cycle of hiring and promoting men to leadership positions.

Women Can "Flat Out" Lead

Women have ran households, taken care of children and husbands, obtained an education, and maintained a career, simultaneously for years, and have done so at a high level. Women are known for and are innately able to lead and handle the emotional pressures of leading due to their nurturing demeanor. They naturally want to serve; look to uplift and inspire others around them and look to "accelerate societal needs".[14]

Additionally, when women are placed in leadership positions, they typically outperform men in basic leadership competencies such as developing others and collaboration and teamwork, according to a Jack Zenger and Joseph Folkman study[15]

---

[14] Llopis, G. (2011). 4 Skills that Give Women a Sustainable Advantage Over Men. Forbes.com. Retrieved from: http://www.forbes.com/sites/glennllopis/2011/08/22/4-skills-that-give-women-a-sustainable-advantage-over-men/

[15] Storrie, M. (2012) The Business Imperative: Recruiting, Developing and Retaining Women in the Workplace. UNC Kenan-Flagler Business School. Retrieved on June 2, 2014 from: http://www.kenan-flagler.unc.edu/executive-development/custom-programs/~/media/3A15E5EC035F420690175C21F9048623.pdf

Why Women are not Advancing in the Workplace?

Being a Working Mom

Women are typically considered the primary caregivers of their families: taking care of children, leaving work when children are ill, tending to the home and performing most of the cooking duties. Women, of course, are also bearing children. Because of this, many women find themselves having to make the difficult decision of either pursuing a career, or being a mother and/or wife. As a woman in her early 30's with no children, I will soon have to face this same question. Do I scale back my career aspirations for children, or can I have it all? Of course, I believe "I can have it all." ☺

Though I am opting to have it all, some women cannot make that same decision. More and more women are delaying having children or not having them at all in order to advance in their career. For example, women who are tenured or advance to leadership roles in academics are more likely to be single, while men who advance to the same position are more likely to be married with children.[16] Why is this? Men are not expected to be single or childless when they are in upper management positions, nor do they typically have to choose between advancing their career or starting a family. How do we change the double standard?

Not Taking Atypical Jobs

When most think of a "female" related job, they would normally note pink collar jobs, such as nursing, administrative positions or customer service. Though these fields may be female dominated, women not going for more atypical jobs is a contributing factor to a lack of representation in leadership roles. Atypical jobs are seen as blue collar jobs, railroad industry, manufacturing or transportation. In addition to these jobs, women are not entering into the STEM field at the rate they

---

[16] Dominici, F., Fried, L. P., & Zeger, S. L. (2009). So few women leaders. Academe

should. The STEM field is Science, Technology, Engineering and Math. Women could be avoiding these fields because they are atypical, because society tells them they cannot succeed in these fields or simply because they are not interested. Avoiding these fields or jobs is immensely causing women to fall behind.

Little or no Mentors or Sponsorships

Leadership's Got Everything to Do With It [17] states it is imperative to have a sponsor in the workplace. Furthermore, sponsors "suggest [their] mentee for leadership roles and promotions".[18] Mentors can additionally contribute to a woman's success, as they provide advice and guidance for a healthy professional and personal life. Despite this, some women are not seeking mentors or sponsors in the workplace. Women who do not have mentors or sponsors typically do not network within their organization. This can be attributed to not taking the initiative to build relationships within the company or simply not understanding how to seek out a mentor or sponsor. Furthermore, some women may not understand how essential a mentor or sponsor can be to their career.

Lack of Preparation and Training

Many trainings and education associated with leadership development for women focus on C-level executives, with limited training for women before they are promoted to this level. With a lack of female executives in the workplace, how are women in lower level positions being trained and prepared for leadership roles? The lack of preparation and other training opportunities serve as a disadvantage for women who have leadership aspirations. If a company is not supporting women with education and preparation opportunities, where are they to go to receive it? Traditional school (MBA)? External workshops, classes or certifications?

---

[17] Brooks (2014) *Leadership's Got Everything to Do With It: Women's Guide to the Sustainable Leader and Organization*. Atlanta, GA. LaKisha C. Brooks
[18] Ibid

Companies Are Not Promoting Women

One of most common reasons women are not advancing in the workplace is because companies are not promoting them. Women are not considered for leadership and decision making roles; furthermore, their work is overlooked and not recognized. In some cases, a company may ask a woman to train a man for a new position-a position she too applied for and was not hired. This act reflects an image that women are qualified to train a man for a particular role, but are not qualified to actually perform the job. Additionally, this can certainly demotivate women and discourage them from applying to leadership positions.

When we look at the number of women in C-level positions, women on boards and women in other decision making roles, it is evident companies are doing a poor job of promoting women. Some companies have no women on their board or women in C-level roles. There is no excuse for this disparaging situation.

The notion of not promoting women or a lack of women in leadership roles goes beyond Corporate America. This is a predicament occurring in all fields, sectors and industries, including government and entertainment.

How Can We Help Advance Women?

Now that it has been determined that there is a need for women in leadership roles, a plan can be put in place to eradicate this problem. One of the responsibilities of advancing women falls on women themselves. There are a number of things that women can do to position themselves for leadership and decision making positions.

Take Initiatives

"It's better to beg for forgiveness than ask for permission." This should be the attitude for women in the workplace. Do not wait to be asked, just do it!!!

When an opportunity to show their leadership and management ability presents itself, women should take it. This can include leading a project, initiating change or simply offering ideas. Showing initiative is a sure fire way to get noticed in the workplace. In addition, try to handle and remedy problems without being assisted. This shows great critical thinking and problem solving skills, both of which are critical skills for a leader.

Though a woman should show initiative, she should be careful with how she shows it. Providing cookies and snacks within the office is not the type of initiative a woman should show. This can be seen as "soft" and more of an assistant's role. These are not the qualities that most companies look for when looking for potential leaders and decision makers. They want tough, assertive individuals who can take charge and show initiative.

Showing initiative also includes asking for and seeking promotion opportunities. Speaking with human resources or hiring managers regarding job openings is an effective method to seek new opportunities within an organization. Human resource departments are typically informed of new positions before they are posted internally or externally. Once a woman has this information, she can use it to leverage herself and gain an advantage over potential candidates.

Training, Education and Classes

There is nothing more valuable than an education. Women can position themselves for success with continuous education in their respective fields. Continuous education does not always mean in a traditional setting such as a bachelor's or master's degree; it can simply entail attending training classes, workshops or certifications. These forms of education should focus on particular areas or skill sets related to and needed to advance one's career. Some companies allot funds for employees to further their education.

Take Atypical Jobs

When offered an opportunity to get into an industry that is abnormal for a woman, take it. Try blue collar industries such as transportation or gasoline/petroleum. In addition to these industries, women, should get more involved in STEM jobs, which are predominately male industries. Women interested in these fields can find themselves receiving immense incentives including scholarships, internships/externships and increased career options. Going against the norm and obtaining an atypical job shows resiliency, tenacity and fearlessness- all qualities needed to be an effective leader in high pressured situations.

Find a Sponsor

In order for women to position themselves for success within an organization, a sponsor is necessary. Women should find a sponsor two hierarchical levels above them who can assist in the advancement of their career. Finding the right sponsor includes networking within the organization, learning different personalities, and knowing how potential sponsors are aligned with their overall career goals. Once a sponsor is selected, set assign time to discuss goals and devise a strategic plan to achieve those goals.

Be Confident and Comfortable with Having Success

As simple as it may sound, being confident is one of the biggest ways a woman can position herself for leadership and important decision making roles within an organization. Being confident entails accepting success and not apologizing for it. When being recognized for accomplishments, some women, instead of simply saying "thank you" with their heads held high wearing a smile, meekly downplay their accolades with justifications such as "well, it wasn't that great" or "it was only because of this or that". This attitude does not focus on the success itself, but rather on the justifications. ***Just take the compliments, smile and be quiet!*** Businesses look for self-assured, proven leaders who know they are great at specifics tasks and can confidently lead a team and manage an organization. What part of "it wasn't that great" screams "I am confident, and I can handle success?"

Work Effectively with Other Women

With few women in important decision making and leadership roles, it is imperative that they work together to help leverage an advantage in the workplace. Unfortunately, this is not always the case. Many women state they would rather work under or alongside a man than a woman. But why? Perhaps, it is due to the shortage of leadership roles and opportunities for advancement for women in the workplace, and everyone is vying for those few chances. It is similar to a pageant where there are many qualified, beautiful and experienced women competing for ONE crown. In this case however, it is not a crown, but a board seat, C-level position or any other decision making role.

In order to work effectively with other women, a woman must first understand that despite the gender gap for leadership and decision making positions, she must not view other women as competition, but rather allies fighting for the same cause. There should be a sense of "sisterhood", as most women are striving for the same goal-to see a change in the face of leadership in America.

In the book, *Women's Code*, author Sophia Nelson offers five tips on how women can better work together in the workplace.

1. Steer clear of women who "don't do" women friends
2. Collaborate and share

3.   Be a mentor

4.   It's reciprocal

5.   Be willing to have "courageous" conversations [19]

Company and Government Influence and Involvement

Though women have a hand in their own success and ability to obtain leadership positions, companies and the government can greatly influence change.

As previously discussed, one of the greatest reasons women are not advancing is because they are trying to balance work and their personal lives. In order to retain more women in the workplace and not force them chose between family and a career, companies and the government can:

1.   **Allow women to work remotely**

Because of today's growing technological world, companies are electing to allow employees to work remotely. They are able to complete the same tasks, in the same time frame, but do it from a home office or any other remote location. The company is able to save money and employees are able to enjoy working in their pajamas. Companies should take the same approach with working mothers. If her job does not require her to be in an office 40 hours a week, then the more plausible option should be to allow her to work remotely. This will allow her to stay home with her children or be home for important activities, while still fulfilling her professional obligations. Moreover, offering flexible scheduling may be a suitable alternative.

---

[19] Nelson, S. (2014). *The Woman Code: 20 Powerful Keys to Unlock Your Life*. Grand Rapids, MI. Baker Publishing Group

2. **Allow women to have more PAID maternity days**

The Family and Medical Leave Act of 1993 states mothers are entitled to 12 weeks of unpaid leave, but only if the employee has been at the business at least 12 months, and worked at least 1,250 hours over the past 12 months and works for a company that has more than 50 employees.[20]

There are some states that have added provisions to the federal legislation to accommodate new mothers; some states even offer paid maternity leave through Short Term Disability Insurance or other sources.

3. **Offer men more paternity days to assist women with childcare duties**

More and more men are assuming child rearing duties in the homes and need extra time to assist mothers. Companies should recognize this and make certain provisions for men. This will encourage a better work-life balance for working mothers.

4. **Provide onsite child care facilities**

Many working mothers love going into an office every day; they love the bond with co-workers and enjoy the team comradery. There are even those who, because of the nature of their job, have to physically go into a building or office. In order to accommodate the working mother, companies can provide onsite child care facilities. Women would be able to take their children to work and alleviate issues concerning child care providers. Some child care providers' operating hours are limited, having mothers scramble to leave work early to ensure their children are picked up before accruing after-hour child care fees.

---

[20] The Family and Medical Leave Act of 1993.(1993). Wage and Hour Division (WHD). United States Department of Labor

In addition to accommodating the working mother, the government can mandate companies to consider at least one qualified woman for any open board seat, or create a quota system. This process or something similar has been introduced or is in practice in number of other countries such as Brazil, Germany and France.

Furthermore, the government can offer tax credits to companies who hire a certain number or a percentage of women to upper leadership positions. There are some who do not agree with government influence in order to create or implement change, but the change has to start somewhere, so why not our government?

The 4 R's to Advancing Women in the Workplace

Though there is no clear formula to advance women in the workplace, there are a few simple steps that companies can take.

-**Recruit** –Companies should invest time and money to recruit qualified women who they deem as potential leaders. They may even recruit experienced, successful women to fill executive level roles or board seats. This means targeting qualified women via hiring an outside recruiting company, searching for talent on websites such as Indeed.com or LinkedIn.com or looking for high performing women within their own organization.

-**Refine**-Once companies have recruited qualified women, they should continue to hone their talents, skills and abilities. This includes providing training, education, workshops and other tools to help with their female employees' professional development. Other methods to refining talent are performance assessments and on-going feedback. A company's ultimate goal should be grooming a woman for a leadership role. When a woman is promoted to a leadership position, she too, will need continuous on-going training in various areas to prepare her for C-level roles.

-**Recognize**-If a female employee does a great job, recognize her! This can be as simple as providing a certificate of achievement, giving a compliment or considering her for a management position. Women in the workplace want to feel they are appreciated and their work is noticed. Do not give someone else credit for the work she has done.

-**Retain**-One of the areas that most companies fail in advancing women is simply not retaining them. If women feel they are not being groomed, are not being recognized, and have no shot of moving up in a company, they will leave. They will either leave to work for someone else or "standition" to their own company.

Summary

Despite obtaining over 50 percent of all entry level positions, women are still not advancing to leadership and decision making roles at the same rate as men. Additionally, women are still underrepresented on boards for many Standard and Poor (S&P) 500 companies.

The need for women in leadership and decision making roles is critical to the United States workforce and economy. Women offer a unique perspective, are emotionally intelligent, make most of the purchasing decisions within most households, and they can "flat out" lead.

Reasons for a lack of women in leadership roles vary from companies not recognizing or promoting women to a lack of training, education or sponsorship.

Knowing what the problem is and why there is a problem can help change the face of leadership and the United States can start to take a "stiletto step" in the right direction.

Chapter 2

Unequal Pay in the Workplace and the Consequences for Women and Society

By: Latasha Kinnard
Financial Freedom Fighter
CEO & Chief Coach, Start Young Financial Group
Former analyst managing $100 million budgets, now helping people like you.

Who Runs the World?

Girls. That is what American recording artist, Beyonce, tells millions of her adoring fans in her song "Run the World (Girls)"[21] that was released in 2011. The song gained notoriety in pop culture as a feminist anthem and reached number 29 on the Billboard's Hot 100 list. The song is commendable in that it is able to emphatically rally women to unapologetically assert their worth. However, the empowering lyrics speak to a vision that is not yet reality.

In the 21st century, we would like to believe that equality between the sexes is an indisputable fact that does not require discussion. Yet, it is not. Inequality in pay between men and women is not a new cultural phenomenon in America. According to the International Labor Organization, in 1979 women made only 62% as much as men[22]. Today, women make 78% as much as men as calculated by the Department of Labor[23], and while this is a 16 percentage point improvement, you will not find too many women celebrating. Instead,

---

[21] Metrolyrics, Run the World (Girls) (New York: Columbia Records, 2011), http://www.metrolyrics.com/run-the-world-lyrics-beyonce.html
[22] Women in the Labor Force: A Databook. (2013).Retrieved May 12, 2015, from http://www.bls.gov/cps/wlf-databook-2012.pdf
[23] NWLC calculations from U.S. Census Bureau, Current Population Survey, 2014 Annual Social and Economic Supplement [hereinafter CPS, 2014 ASEC], Table PINC-05: Work Experience in 2013 – People 15 Years Old and Over by Total Money Earnings in 2013, Age, Race, Hispanic Origin, and Sex, available at http://www.census.gov/hhes/www/cpstables/032014/perinc/toc.htm

women are growing impatient regarding the evident stagnation that has characterized the last decade. Since 2003, the National Women's Law Center reports that the amount women earn in comparison to men has continued to hover around the 77% mark, with no signs of improving[24]. How could it improve without the support of governing bodies to consistently enforce the equal pay legislation that has been on the books since 1963? So while women, have in theory, been granted access to equal pay, this does not align with the reality of wage distribution.

Women are tired of being appeased with powerless laws and feel good anthems when nothing is actually changing. The women in today's workforce are becoming increasingly aware of their worth and how important equal pay is to their financial future. Women literally cannot afford to remain silent in the face of wage stagnation because the effects are far reaching, impacting more than just half the population. Since women are the cornerstone of society, caregivers in families, and an essential partner in the home, anything that negatively impacts the lives and financial well-being of women will surely reverberate through society at large.

Because of the inherent interconnectedness of the issue of women's pay and the well-being of society at large, it is hard to imagine that the discussion is largely framed as part of a feminist agenda that only serves women. On the surface, the issue is one of gender inequality, making it difficult to approach the subject without making sweeping generalizations. In fact, generalizations are almost inherent, as we address differences between men and women, two distinct and heterogeneous communities. Yet, there is a way to thoughtfully and thoroughly examine the existence of pervasive financial equalities between men and women with as much integrity, analysis, and critical observation as possible. Additionally, we will demonstrate that

---

[24] The Wage Gap is Stagnant for Nearly a Decade. (2014). Retrieved May 12, 2015, from http://www.nwlc.org/resource/wage-gap-stagnant-nearly-decade

although gender is of central significance, the problem impacts men, women, and children. This chapter will explore the cultural underpinnings of unequal pay, the consequences for women and society, and most importantly, how women can ensure their financial well-being in the face of such challenges. So, while Beyonce might insist that girls run the world, James Brown's assertion that "This is a man's world,[25]" seems more factually accurate. However, that will not stop women from "ringing the alarm" and sounding off against gender inequality, especially when it impacts checkbooks and general well-being.

Cultural Underpinnings for Unequal Pay

The 1960s were a time of transformation for women. As a group, women decided that they were not going to take it anymore. They bonded together to demand equal pay, an end to domestic violence, consequences for sexual harassment, and an opportunity for advancement in the workforce. USA Today wrote an article about it a few years ago titled, "The 1960s: A Decade of Change for Women"[26]. The article captures the contradictions inherent in a decade where women were fighting for equal rights, while men artistically asserted their power to the masses through television. These were certainly confusing times, and the confusion would not stop in this decade. It would continue well into the 21st century.

Inequality between men and women did not begin in the workplace, but is the manifestation of deep seated gender roles that started in the home. While some scholars and statisticians argue about the reality and nuances of gender inequality, The American Sociological Review's "Sex

---

[25] Metro lyrics. It's a Man's Man's Man's World (New York: King Records, 1966), http://www.metrolyrics.com/its-a-mans-mans-world-lyrics-james-brown.html

[26] Walsh, K. (2010). The 1960s: A Decade of Change for Women. Retrieved April 17, 2015, from http://www.usnews.com/news/articles/2010/03/12/the-1960s-a-decade-of-change-for-women

and Authority in the Workplace: The Causes of Sexual Inequality"[27] accepts it as fact and explores the causes. The discussion starts with the impact of traditional gender roles. Authors Wolf and Fligstein state that "while men have obtained power throughout their positions in the work setting, women's power traditionally has been derived from their roles in the family."[28] This statement is an obvious truth, but still a necessary reminder. In a modern society where feminism is a prominent topic of conversation and gender roles are frequently challenged, it is easy to forget that just a few decades ago it was a widely accepted fact that a woman's place was in the home. Today, women are able to work in any field that they choose and are going to college in record numbers. This easily blurs the lines between what is possible for women and what is customary.

Our current cultural backdrop for feminism is very different from what it was in decades past. It is not a complete exaggeration to say that modern feminists commonly connect through witty buzz feed articles, sarcastic infographics on Facebook, and occasionally from textbooks that tell of a history that most modern day women cannot connect to. Today, feminism bleeds out of the ivory tower and into pop culture. While the Women's Suffrage Movement demonstrates blatant injustice toward women, it might not easily connect with young women today, who find it difficult to draw inspiration from a struggle they never knew, especially when day to day experiences engender false security in an equality that does not really exist. With the Women's Suffrage and "bra-burning" movements far behind us, today's feminists focus a large portion of their energy on agency, body positivity, and the ability to walk down the street without being harassed. All of these topics are important and deserving of attention, but it certainly draws a stark contrast between what women were fighting for in the early 20th century compared to now. Thus, it might be easier for the modern

---

[27] Wolf, W., & Fligstein, N. (1979). Sex and Authority in the Workplace: The Causes of sexual inequality. Retrieved April 13, 2015, from http://www.jstor.org/stable/2094507?seq=1#page_scan_tab_contents
[28] Ibid

women to fall for the lull of unfulfilled promises where we have the appearance of equality, but lack true access.

In the fight for equality of the sexes, it is undeniable that women have made strides. The cultural advancements on this front are not to be undervalued. As a society, we went from having women be viewed as the property of their husbands, to change agents in our society. The growth is commendable. Yet, there is still so much room to continue growing. The fact that women have come so far could in fact be one reason why the wage gap has remained stagnant and not much has been done about it. It is possible to acknowledge improvements and still demand greater change. If we are to challenge and dismantle the impact of patriarchal views on the role of women in society, we have to remember and acknowledge that there is still a residue of the concepts that gave rise to traditional gender roles. This residue that is left over from decades and centuries of women being considered as children has deeply impacted the people and institutions that govern our country. It is these very institutions and power structures that have allowed the pay gap to remain exactly where it is for so many years, and if we are to change it, we have to look beyond what we have been given and design systems that are well suited to meet the needs of men and women.

Women all over the world desire to receive equal pay for equal work and be viewed as valued and contributing members of society. Often, we find that women are denigrated and devalued in our culture which makes it easier for the individuals that operate within our institutions to justify unequal treatment and compensation.

The Consequences of Unequal Pay for Women and Society

Unequal pay in the workplace has far reaching implications. In particular, three challenges consistently come up when considering how the wage gap impacts the lives of women. When women workers are not paid equal wages they have less money to access for retirement, less money for healthcare expenses later in life, and they are less able to support their families with their income contributions. This demonstrates that while women are the most vocal about the quest to achieve equal pay, this is not just a woman's issue as it very directly impacts children and families. Let's explore these three points more deeply:

1. When women do not receive equal pay, they have less money available for retirement.

When it comes to retirement in general, over 70% of Americans are not ready[29]. While this is an epidemic of mass proportions, the issue is amplified for women who only receive three quarters on the dollar when compared with their male counterparts. Unequal pay not only means less income, but it also means less savings and less social security money available at the time of retirement. According to the Washington Post, "women retire with two-thirds the savings of men."[30] This is especially problematic when compounded with the fact that women on average live longer than men and have higher medical bills. This is not a problem that can be fixed simply with a better saving strategy, but must also be supported by acknowledging the impact of the wage gap and then doing the policy work to change it.

2. When women do not receive equal pay, they struggle to make ends meet.

In the past, it was easy to justify the wage gap by making the assumption that men were more likely to have families to support. According to the Single Mother Guide, 83% of single parent

---

[29] Marksjarvis, G. (2015). Americans ill-prepared for retirement, survey finds. Retrieved April 13, 2015, from http://www.chicagotribune.com/business/yourmoney/ct-marksjarvis-0422-biz-20150421-column.html
[30] Krawcheck, S. (2015). Why the Retirement Crisis is Also a Women's Crisis. Retrieved April 27, 2015, from http://www.washingtonpost.com/news/get-there/wp/2015/04/24/why-the-retirement-savings-crisis-is-also-a-womens-crisis/

households are headed by women with a median income of $26,000.[31] Additionally, the U.S Census Bureau notes that about 17.4 million children in the United States are raised with no father in the home, with 45% living below the poverty line.[32] This paints a dreary picture not only for women, but also for their children. The inequality that has plagued and continues to plague women in the workplace cannot be considered within a silo because women are literally the birthplace of the next generation. Whatever happens to children will inevitably affect their children. While men might be able to distance themselves from responsibility, this is an option that is rarely afforded to women due to the nature of birthing and pregnancy.

When it comes to child rearing and responsibility in America, many fathers do take an active approach to fatherhood. For those who do not, the buck almost always stops with the mother. This certainly seems natural, but it also exacerbates the income disparities that are caused by this very same gender bias that says women are more suited to activities in the home. There is a space for understanding the role of mothers as caregivers, but there must also be recognition that the structure of the workplace must change to equally accommodate women and provide them with the equal pay that is necessary.

3.   When women do not receive equal pay, even two parent homes suffer.

In 2013, 1.4 million families relied on the woman as the sole breadwinner, and countless more counted on the woman as a contributor.[33] This shows that even when a man is the primary breadwinner or simply an equal contributor, there is still a huge negative impact that arises from women being denied equal pay. No

---

[31] Single Mother Guide. (2015). Retrieved May 15, 2015, from https://singlemotherguide.com/single-mother-statistics/
[32] U.S. Census Bureau – Table C2. Household Relationship and Living Arrangements of Children Under 18 Years, by Age and Sex: 2014
[33] Dawn (n.d.).Single Mother Guide. Retrieved on May 2,2015, from https://singlemotherguide.com/single-mother-statistics

matter what their home life is like, women must demand equal pay first and foremost because it is a right, but also because it affects their children and their spouses in the long run. Essentially, the pay gap is responsible for entire families having less money to live on which is ultimately going to decrease the overall wealth potential of the family. Outside of what will happen to the family, there are some very interesting affects for women specifically. Our current economy still has problem, and as it stands, 76% of Americans are not prepared for retirement.[34] What do you think happens when an entire half of the United States is not compensated fairly and is expected to outlive their partners? It does not take a mathematician to understand that women are poised to run out of money. In order to combat this, we need some serious strategies in place that do more than just tell women to save more. We need real institutional change to occur that will level the playing field.

One might assume that men are more likely to be in positions of power because they are better suited to produce results in high powered and rigorous environments, but that would be an incorrect assumption. Kevin O'leary, from the hit show *Shark Tank*, recently analyzed his investment portfolio looking to identify the common denominator between his most profitable companies. His team found it: Every single profitable company in the "shark's" portfolio was run by a woman. O'leary asked one of his female CEOs why she thought women were so successful at running profitable companies. The word "multitasking" came up, and she said, "want something done, give it to a busy mom"[35]. It is undeniable that women possess many skills that would make them well suited for positions of power and their unequal representation, and unequal pay is indicative of a far reaching problem.

---

[34] Marksjarvis, G. (2015). Americans ill-prepared for retirement, survey finds. Retrieved April 13, 2015, from http://www.chicagotribune.com/business/yourmoney/ct-marksjarvis-0422-biz-20150421-column.html

[35] Mulshine, M. (2015). Kevin O'Leary of 'Shark Tank' invests in 27 companies and says the only ones making money have female CEOs. Retrieved May 19, 2015, from http://www.businessinsider.com/kevin-olearys-female-ceos-make-all-the-money-2015-5

How Women Can Ensure Financial Well Being in the Face of Pay Inequality.

Women are an indomitable force in the workplace and in our society as a whole. Nevertheless, they do not have the luxury of waiting for equal pay to secure our financial futures. Like many other things in this world, women must figure out how to dominate even in the face of adversity, which is something they have become very good at. Here are 5 tips that every woman should adhere to as closely as possible in order to secure long term financial freedom.

1. **Create a Budget**

If women are serious about taking control of their finances and not being hold to any person or system to make it happen, it must start with a budget. A solid budget is the engine to every good financial plan and yet, only 30% of Americans have one.[36] Well for women, this is not an option, but a necessity to thrive in a system where the odds are not in their favor.

A good budget is made up of four major components, which include income, expenses, savings, and investments. Every single category is critical and should be studied and understood intimately. Many people do not have a laser like awareness of their finances, which makes it impossible for them to improve their financial standing. Women must know how much money they have coming in every month while also managing what they do with it. It stands to reason that if one is unaware of how much money they have coming in, it is going to be challenging to allocate it properly. This is why clarifying income must be the first consideration of every financial plan. From there, all expenses must be taken into account. This includes bills, debt, and other day to day expenditures. It would also be wise to write down the

---

[36] Jacobe, D. (2013). One in Three Americans Prepare a Detailed Household Budget. Retrieved April 14th, 2015 from http://www.gallup.com/poll/162872/one-three-americans-prepare-detailed-household-budget.aspx

dates that bills are due in order to be aware of when financial transactions will take place. After concentrating on expenses, women should shift their attention to how much money they are saving and for what end. Finally, they should make sure that they take advantage of the company's 401k or 403b plan if they have one. These are retirement vehicles that allow a person to invest directly from their paycheck. Usually, companies will match an employee contribution up to a certain percentage. It is recommended that women invest into their employer sponsored retirement account up to the amount that their company is willing to match. Women can connect with their Human Resource Specialist to get more details on how this can work in their favor because ultimately, it is free money that they do not want to leave on the table. By focusing on setting up each portion of the budget correctly, women will be able to create a realistic plan to stay on top of their financial goals.

2.   **Save Relentlessly**

Saving is the third component of a successful budget. Being relentless and insistent in saving for the future, is a critical component of financial success for women who are suffering major financial setbacks due to unequal pay. As legislators, policy makers, and advocates continue to make noise and fight to close the wage gap, increasing the amount of money saved now will ensure that today's working woman is able to take care of herself and her family in the event of an emergency. Additionally, planning for the future is an often overlooked way to build wealth. It reduces the need to pull from retirement which dramatically improves long term wealth potential. Savings can be created for everything, from cars and homes to vacations and clothes. Saving allows women to make a financial plan for the things that matter to them most. That way, they can engage and indulge without feeling guilty.

3.   Double Investments

With single moms having a median income of $26,000[37], it is undoubtedly difficult to find the financial resources to save and invest, and yet, they must. Women face a multitude of challenges when it comes to preparing for a stable financial future. In addition to operating with less financial resources to take care of present day expenses, money must also be set aside for long term investment goals and retirement. Retirement planning is an issue that plagues all Americans on a large scale, but it is especially challenging for women who are earning an income equal to only three quarters of every male dollar. Still, resting in the truth of inequality will not generate income or benefits during retirement. So the question becomes: What are women going to do about it? In this situation, drastic times call for drastic measures, and although the following call to action is difficult, it is also necessary. In order to plan for a stable retirement, women not only need to start investing, but they should also consider doubling their investment contributions in their 401K or general investment vehicle while also maxing out their Individual Retirement Account.

A 401K (or 403b) is an employer sponsored retirement account where both employee and employer have the opportunity to contribute. A general investment account is something that women can invest in on their own, or with the help of a financial coach, or a financial advisor. An individual retirement account is another type of retirement account that comes with tax benefits, but a person can only contribute a certain maximum each year. Right now, the maximum is $5500, but this changes frequently depending on the tax year.

 When it comes to doubling an investment, women should first consider investing up to the company match, which was explained previously. Next, they should focus on "maxing out" their IRA. This simply means contributing as much as the IRS will allow based on the

---

[37] Dawn. (n.d.) Single Mother Statistics. Single Mother Guide. Retrieved on May 3, 2015 from: https://singlemotherguide.com/

maximum for that year. Finally, once they have leveraged both of those vehicles, a general investment account is where they would put the rest. When it comes to your financial planning, there is no one-size-fits-all approach. Women can connect with financial professionals in their area, and they can reach out to human resources within their company to maximize what they get from their employer, and what they are able to do on their own. Find a plan that works, and stick with it.

In some ways, doubling investment contributions might seem like an extreme plan, but a lower earning potential automatically puts women at risk for a shortfall of funds in retirement. For example, current FICA rates are at 6.2%[38] for all Americans. FICA is the amount of a paycheck that is taken out for social security and Medicare. Employees contribute, and the employer contributes. If a person's overall income is lower, this means that both the employee and their employer are contributing a smaller percentage for the employee, which could ultimately mean a smaller payout. When an employer contributes to an employee's retirement, it is also based on their income. A smaller income means a smaller contribution from both employee and employer. There are several small instances of how the wage gap impacts a woman's future, and they add up. So doubling their investment is a way to hedge women's bets against the prospect of lower wages.

4. Get Life Insurance on Your Significant Other

According to the worldwide research, learning and development organization LIMRA's study, "Trends in Life Insurance Ownership Study" only 44% of US households had individual life insurance even though over 11 million women are widowed in the United States every year.[39] Since women are making less money and living longer than their

---

[38] U.S. Department of the Treasury, Internal Revenue Service, Topic 751. Washington, DC: 2015. Retrieved on May 7, 2015, from: http://www.irs.gov/taxtopics/tc751.html
[39] Facts About Life 2013. Retrieved May 10, 2015, from
http://www.limra.com/uploadedFiles/limracom/Posts/PR/LIAM/PDF/Facts-Life-2013.pdf

significant others, this paints a very clear picture around the need for women to have life insurance on their husbands. It is extremely important that women are protected in the event that they lose financial support, whether their husband is the main breadwinner or a significant contributor to the finances.

5. Demand a Raise

Knowing that women are paid significantly less than men, it is smart to position themselves to receive what they already deserve. This means preparing for performance reviews proactively, keeping their resumes updated, and acquiring skills that make them even more marketable. Women should make sure that they are always an asset to your company or organization. Once they make sure their presence is invaluable, they can then ask for the pay they deserve. Women are less likely to negotiate than men. Changing this one factor could help women close the wage gap so that they can earn what they deserve.

Summary

It is unfortunate in the 21st century that we are still talking about inequality, yet here we are. On the journey to receive equal pay to ensure financial well-being, women need to remember to value their womanhood. Women make an irreplaceable contribution to society. It is not women's job to change core values to fit into the workplace. Instead, every woman should continue to show up in full female glory to remind all parties in the workplace that they are here to stay and have skills that are invaluable to the success of the companies they serve.

Chapter 3

Demanding and Earning Respect in the Workplace

By: Sabrina Brawner
Writer and Franchise Based Business Owner, The Weave Shop-Lithonia

History of Women in the Workplace

Women have always had an undeniably important role in American life. Although early on, this importance was mainly expressed through homemaking roles such as cooking, cleaning, and sewing, we should not be fooled about the level of strength, tenacity, and dedication it took to perform these roles—especially in a world without the many conveniences, and technology we enjoy today. Much of this work took long hours and painstaking attention to detail to complete, yet women helped to make sure their families were clothed and fed, and that the home and gardens, or farms were taken care of. In the 16th and 17th century, the jobs women took on outside the home were still based around clothing maintenance services, cooking and cleaning. According to the article, "A History of Women's Jobs[40]," these jobs included work as, "tailoresses, milliners, dyers, shoemakers, and embroiderers …washerwomen …brewers, bakers or confectioners. Women also sold foodstuffs in the streets. Other women were midwives."

Yet despite the contributions women made to the family, home life, and the "early workplace," because of the patriarchal structure of society, they lacked many of the rights that would help them to branch out into more unconventional lines of work such as medicine, science, law, and teaching. "In every state, the legal status of free women depended upon marital status," according to the essay, *The Legal Status*

---

[40] A History of Women's Job. (n.d.). Retrieved August 24, 2015, from http://www.localhistories.org/womensjobs.html

of Women, 1776-1830[41], by Marylynn Salmon . Salmon states that, married women, "still had legal rights but no longer had autonomy."[42] Instead, married women were subject to a common-law concept called coverture.

> *West's Encyclopedia of American Law* defines coverture as:
>
> The protection and control of a woman by her husband that gave rise to various rights and obligations. Upon marriage, a Husband and Wife were said to have acquired unity of person that resulted in the husband having numerous rights over the property of his wife and in the wife being deprived of her power to enter into contracts or to bring lawsuits as an independent person.[43]

Essentially, whatever assets or property a woman entered into a marriage with, became "theirs," but under the sole power and control of the husband. Unmarried women or widows "had a legal right to live where they pleased and to support themselves in any occupation that did not require a license or a college degree restricted to males[44]," According to Salmon, "single women could enter into contracts, buy and sell real estate, or accumulate personal property.[45]" Although it

---

[41] Salmon, M. The Legal Status of Women, 1776–1830. (n.d.). Retrieved August 24, 2015, from http://www.gilderlehrman.org/history-by-era/womens-history/essays/legal-status-women-1776–1830
[42] Ibid
[43] Coverture. (n.d.) West's Encyclopedia of American Law, edition 2. (2008). Retrieved August 23 2015 from http://legal-dictionary.thefreedictionary.com/coverture
[44] Salmon, M. The Legal Status of Women, 1776–1830. (n.d.). Retrieved August 24, 2015, from http://www.gilderlehrman.org/history-by-era/womens-history/essays/legal-status-women-1776–1830
[45] Ibid

seemed more liberating to be a single woman at this time, it was a sort of social embarrassment. Societal pressures pushed the unmarried woman into marrying, and the widowed woman into re-marrying as quickly as possible. Despite this pressure, ironically, it was through becoming a widow, or not marrying, that women obtained the freedom to work on their own terms. Some of these women became the earliest American business owners, working in businesses they inherited, or opened up themselves.

The article, "Women and Labor in Early America," by Jone Johnson Lewis, asserts that "in the 1840s and 1850s as the Industrial Revolution and factory labor took hold in the United States, more women went to work outside the home."[46] During this time there was a need for families to increase their household incomes, and Lewis states that, "factory owners hired women and children when they could, because they could pay lower wages to women and children than to men.[47]" As the United States continued to make industrial strides, the female labor force slowly increased, filled with women who were working because they had to. This included single and married African American women who, "since the late nineteenth century…participated in the labor force at a rate higher than that of any other group of American women[48]," according to the article, "Women in the Labor Force." By the 1920s, the numbers of working women were still relatively low, and opportunities were likely to fall under the category of "women jobs," such as, "teachers, social workers, nurses, and librarians[49]". Furthermore, due to "the rise of the corporate office," during this period, jobs as "typists, filing clerks, stenographers, and even some

---

[46] Lewis, J. (n.d.). Women and Labor in Early America. Retrieved August 24, 2015, from http://womenshistory.about.com/od/worklaborunions/a/early_america.htm
[47] Ibid
[48] Women in the Labor Force. (n.d.). Retrieved August 24, 2015, from http://www.anb.org/cush_wlabor.html
[49] Working and Voting -- Women in the 1920s. (n.d.). Retrieved August 24, 2015, from http://www.americanhistoryusa.com/working-voting-women-1920s/

secretarial roles all became possibilities for the ambitious young woman."[50]

World War II offered many opportunities for women to work outside the home, and they entered the workforce in large numbers. Many women served in the military and others filled jobs that were left vacant by men who had gone to war. The article, "American Women in World War II," states that "between 1940 and 1945, the female percentage of the U.S. workforce increased from 27 percent to nearly 37 percent, and by 1945 nearly one out of every four married women worked outside the home.[51]" Despite America's need for women to work during this time, and despite the importance of the work women were doing, pay was largely unequal. Women made no more than "50 percent of male wages.[52]"

We have seen more women get appointed to leadership positions within Fortune 500 Companies, and we saw Ursula Burns become the first black female CEO of a Fortune 500 company. Countless others hold managerial or directorial positions in other companies. Women have also been major contributors in the areas of law, science, math, and technology. Additionally, women have entered the world of politics and left their mark as judges, representatives, and senators, and we have even seen a female Vice Presidential candidate.

Relevance of Respect in Today's Workplace

Today's professional woman has a unique position in the workplace. Women are more educated and are heading more companies than ever before. Women make up more than half of the nation's college students, and are more likely to go on to get Master's degrees and doctorates than men. The face of today's CEO is also changing. There

---

[50] Ibid
[51] American Women in World War II. (n.d.). Retrieved August 24, 2015, from http://www.history.com/topics/world-war-ii/american-women-in-world-war-ii
[52] Ibid

are 9.1 million women owned businesses in the United States,[53] and they "employ 35% more people than all of the Fortune 500 companies combined"[54], which are headed mostly by men. This proves women are really becoming a huge management force. Despite this, women still have to fight for respect amongst their peers, especially the male counterparts. Even though women are making huge strides, it is clear that women are still fighting to gain respect in the workplace. This chapter explores different forms of disrespect, ways to demand and earn respect, and the benefits of being respected in the workplace.

Defining Respect and its Role in Human Psychology/Sociology

Respect is defined as the feeling or understanding that someone or something is important, serious, etc., and should be treated in an appropriate way.[55] When we respect someone or something we hold them or it in high esteem for some admirable quality. Respect makes us considerate, and it causes us to adjust our behavior so that our actions are approved. Who or what we show respect to will be based on several factors, including our morals, our motivations and goals, and how others show respect. Although these things vary depending on culture, upbringing, and socio-economic background, one thing is sure—people know how respect makes them feel. If we can identify the good feelings of self-worth we feel from being respected, then we can also identify the negative feelings that disrespect can cause. Respect is a basic human need. It is directly related to esteem, the fourth level in Maslow's Hierarchy of Needs.[56] Every person wants to be treated in a respectful manner and when that respect is not given, conflicts abound.

---

[53] National Association of Women Business Owners. (n.d.). Retrieved on May 12, 2015, from http://nawbo.org/section_103.cfm
[54] 10 Surprising Statistics on Women in the Workplace | WorkplaceRantings.com. (n.d.). Retrieved on May 1, 2015 from: http://www.workplacerantings.com/10-surprising-statistics-on-women-in-the-workplace
[55] Respect (n.d.). Retrieved on May 20, 2015 , from http://www.merriam-webster.com/dictionary/respect
[56] Maslow's Hierarchy of Needs. (2007). Simply Psychology. Retrieved on April 27, 2015, from http://www.simplypsychology.org/maslow.html

A person can start to feel inferior to others and question their worth. They can become a person who seeks to create their own sense of worth through seeking power, being aggressive at the expense of others, and tearing others down in an attempt to build themselves up. When this occurs, the person may get the respect they are seeking, however it is now built on a flimsy foundation. Furthermore, these people help to perpetuate a cycle of hurt people hurting others. People carry their personalities, character, experiences, and all of the traits that make that make them who they are into every aspect of life. Although there is a standard of professionalism in the workplace, this does not change people, and because of this, issues surrounding respect in the workplace come up often.

Forms of Disrespect in the Workplace

Disrespect in the workplace can take on many forms. Many people are most aware of the blatant forms of disrespect in the workplace. These can take the form of bullying, discrimination and harassment, being left out of meetings, discussions, trainings, and events, and not being recognized for your ideas or achievements. Bullying usually comes up in discussion in relation to school children these days, but it definitely happens in the workplace. It is in fact so prevalent that there is an organization dedicated solely to eradicating bullying in the workplace. Work Place Bullying Institute (WBI) is, "the first and only U.S. organization dedicated to the eradication of workplace bullying that combines help for individuals, research, books, public education, training for professionals-unions-employers, legislative advocacy, and consulting solutions for organizations."[57] They define bullying as "a systematic campaign of interpersonal destruction that jeopardizes your health, your career, and the job you once loved... [It] is a non-physical, non-homicidal form of violence and because it is violence and abusive,

---

[57] Workplace Bullying Institute. (n.d.) Retrieved from on April 17, 2015, from http://www.workplacebullying.org/

emotional harm frequently results."[58] They maintain that workplace bullying experiences have effects both at work and outside of work. WBI lists these examples of what a person can experience at work:

•	You attempt the obviously impossible task of doing a new job without training or time to learn new skills, but that work is never good enough for the boss

•	Surprise meetings are called by your boss with no results other than further humiliation

•	Everything your tormenter does to you is arbitrary and capricious, working a personal agenda that undermines the employer's legitimate business interests

•	Others at work have been told to stop working, talking, or socializing with you

•	You are constantly feeling agitated and anxious, experiencing a sense of doom, waiting for bad things to happen

•	No matter what you do, you are never left alone to do your job without interference

•	People feel justified screaming or yelling at you in front of others, but you are punished if you scream back

•	HR tells you that your harassment isn't illegal, that you have to "work it out between yourselves"

•	You finally, firmly confront your tormentor to stop the abusive conduct and you are accused of harassment

•	You are shocked when accused of incompetence, despite a history of objective excellence, typically by someone who cannot do your job[59]

---

[58] Ibid

- Everyone -- co-workers, senior bosses, HR -- agrees (in person and orally) that your tormentor is a jerk, but there is nothing they will do about it (and later, when you ask for their support, they deny having agreed with you)

- Your request to transfer to an open position under another boss is mysteriously denied

WBI lists these examples of what a person can experience outside of work:

- You feel like throwing up the night before the start of your work week

- Your frustrated family demands that you to stop obsessing about work at home

- Your doctor asks what could be causing your skyrocketing blood pressure and recent health problems, and tells you to change jobs

- You feel too ashamed of being controlled by another person at work to tell your spouse or partner

- All your paid time off is used for "mental health breaks" from the misery

- Days off are spent exhausted and lifeless, your desire to do anything is gone

- Your favorite activities and fun with family are no longer appealing or enjoyable

- You begin to believe that you provoked the workplace cruelty [60]

---

[59] Ibid
[60] Ibid

Most people agree that bullying is detrimental to the objectives of the workplace, but it is much more likely to happen rather than discrimination or sexual harassment because it is legal and not formally regulated.

EEOC.gov is the website for the U.S. Equal Employment Opportunity Commission, and according to their website; the organization was created in the historic Civil Rights Act of 1964. "This Act was an omnibus bill addressing not only discrimination in employment, but also discrimination in voting, public accommodations, and education as well."[61] Discrimination is the practice of unfairly treating a person or group of people differently from other people or groups of people. According to the EEOC, types of discrimination protected by law include the categories of: age, disability, equal pay, genetic information, harassment, national origin, pregnancy, race, religion, sex, and sexual harassment.[62] Because of the audacious and unethical nature of disrespect on these levels, many companies employ strict policies in order to formally protect their employees from the problems and conflicts that they cause. Still many of these policies are in place because of the laws, Acts and organizations created because of conflicts caused by these happenings. Presented below are the terms used by the EEOC to describe discrimination, and the corresponding Act or organization that protects anyone who could possibly face discrimination.

> **Age Discrimination** is treating someone less favorably because of their age.
>
> **Disability Discrimination** is when an employer or other entity covered by the Americans with Disabilities Act or the Rehabilitation Act treats a qualified individual with a disability

---

[61] Discrimination by Type.Types of Discrimination. (n.d.) Retrieved on May 2, 2015, from http://eeoc.gov/laws/types/index.cfm
[62] Ibid

who is an employee or applicant unfavorably because they have a disability.

Equal Pay Discrimination is when The Equal Pay Act is violated, which requires that men and women in the same workplace be given equal pay for equal work. The jobs do not have to be identical, but they must be substantially equal. All forms of pay are covered by this law, including salary, overtime pay, bonuses, stock options, profit sharing and bonus plans, life insurance, vacation and holiday pay, cleaning or gasoline allowances, hotel accommodations, reimbursement for travel expenses, and benefits.

Genetic Discrimination is protected by GINA, or the Genetic Information Nondiscrimination Act of 2008 which prohibits genetic information discrimination. Genetic information includes information about an individual's genetic tests, the genetic tests of family members, or family medical history.

Harassment is a type of discrimination that violates Title VII of the Civil Rights Act of 1964, the Age discrimination in Employment Act of 1967, and the Americans with Disabilities Act of 1990. According to the EEOC, harassment becomes unlawful when 1) enduring the offensive conduct becomes a condition of continued employment; 2) the conduct is severe or pervasive enough to create a work environment that a reasonable person would consider intimidating, hostile, or abusive. Anti-discrimination laws also prohibit harassment against individuals in retaliation for filing a discrimination charge, testifying, or participating in any way in an investigation, proceeding, or lawsuit under these laws; or opposing employment practices that they reasonably believe discriminate against individuals, in violation of these laws.

National Origin Discrimination is when people are treated unfavorably because they are from a particular country or part of the world, because of ethnicity or accent, or because they appear to be of a certain ethnic background, even if they are not.

Pregnancy Discrimination involves treating a woman unfavorably because of pregnancy, childbirth or a medical condition related to pregnancy or childbirth. The PDA or Pregnancy Discrimination Act forbids discrimination based on pregnancy when it comes to any aspect of employment, including hiring, firing, pay, job assignments, promotions, layoff, training, fringe benefits, such as leave and health insurance, and any other term or condition of employment.

Race Discrimination involves treating someone (an applicant or employee) unfavorably because he/she is of a certain race or because of personal characteristics associated with race (such as hair texture, skin color, or certain facial features). Color discrimination involves treating someone unfavorably because of skin color complexion. Race/color discrimination also can involve treating someone unfavorably because the person is married to (or associated with) a person of a certain race or color or because of a person's connection with a race-based organization or group, or an organization or group that is generally associated with people of a certain color. Discrimination can also occur when the victim and the person who inflicted the discrimination are the same race or color.

Religious Discrimination involves treating a person (an applicant or employee) unfavorably because of his or her religious beliefs. The law protects not only people who belong to traditional, organized religions, such as Buddhism, Christianity, Hinduism, Islam, and Judaism, but also others who have sincerely held religious, ethical or moral beliefs.

Religious discrimination can also involve treating someone differently because that person is married to (or associated with) an individual of a particular religion or because of his or her connection with a religious organization or group.

Retaliation All of the laws enforced by the EEOC make it illegal to fire, demote, harass, or otherwise "retaliate" against people (applicants or employees) because they filed a charge of discrimination, because they complained to their employer or other covered entity about discrimination on the job, or because they participated in an employment discrimination proceeding (such as an investigation or lawsuit). For example, it is illegal for an employer to refuse to promote an employee because she filed a charge of discrimination with the EEOC, even if EEOC later determined no discrimination occurred.

Sex Discrimination involves treating someone (an applicant or employee) unfavorably because of that person's sex. Sex discrimination also can involve treating someone less favorably because of his or her connection with an organization or group that is generally associated with people of a certain sex. Discrimination against an individual because that person is transgender is discrimination because of sex in violation of Title VII. This is also known as gender identity discrimination. In addition, lesbian, gay, and bisexual individuals may bring sex discrimination claims. These may include, for example, allegations of sexual harassment or other kinds of sex discrimination, such as adverse actions taken because of the person's non-conformance with sex-stereotypes.

Sexual Harassment is unlawful to harass a person (an applicant or employee) because of that person's sex. Harassment can include "sexual harassment" or unwelcome sexual advances, requests for sexual favors, and other verbal or physical harassment of a sexual nature. Harassment does not have to be of a sexual nature, however, and can include offensive remarks about a person's sex. For example, it is illegal to harass a woman by making offensive comments about women in general. Both victim and the harasser can be either a woman or a man, and the victim and harasser can be the same sex.[63]

Disrespect in the workplace can also be subtle. The more subtle forms are harder to pin down as disrespect, but just as destructive as the blatant forms. This is because with these forms, a person often has to decide for themselves whether or not they are a victim instead of automatically knowing that they are. They are also not immediately backed by the law. If a complaint is made, it is harder for it to be taken seriously and easier for a superior to brush off. It is easy to see that this type of disrespect can take place over longer periods of time without any real repercussions to the aggressor, making navigating the workplace a distressing experience for the victim.

In a post from Cheryl Ragsdale highlights six clues that let you know you have been disrespected including: "Having contempt for, making derogatory comments about, expressing scorn, making derisive comments, [being treated] with disregard, and having disdain for." [64]

> **Contempt** is defined as a feeling that someone or something is not worthy of any respect or approval. In the workplace an example of this would be when a co-worker continues to make snide remarks towards another co-worker directly or indirectly due to a built up resentment of them.
>
> **Derogatory comments** shows disrespect by detracting from the character or standing of something. An example would be a younger minority employee beating older employees in a contest to win a workplace leadership award, being told by a

---

[63] Ibid
[64] Ragsdale, C. (n.d.) Retrieved on May 12, 2015 from: http://www.whodoyourespect.com/withholding-respect-being-disrespected-clues/

peer that they have done a good job and that "their people" would be proud.

Scorn is expressed in the workplace when someone rejects or dismisses a person because they have deemed them unworthy of respect or approval. An example would be a peer dismissing an offer of help on a project from another peer in a way that makes it clear that they don't think highly enough of them to take the assistance.

Derisive comments are made when someone says something to criticize a person in an insulting way. An example would be of an employee named Nancy who earns the office nickname "Negative Nancy," after bringing concerns to a superior.

Disregard is when a person is ignored or treated as being unimportant. This could happen to a person who brings a valid concern to a superior and gets blown off altogether.

Disdain is expressed when someone makes it clear that they have a strong dislike or disapproval for someone or something they do not think deserves respect. An example of this in the workplace is someone rolling their eyes at a person every time they express an opinion during a meeting or other work event.[65]

Most people with workplace experience will have experienced disrespect on this level at some point. It can lead to discrimination, but often rides the borderline, and only if it is extreme, will only it result in the offender being disciplined. Often disrespect can be identified if it makes someone respond in an offended or emotional way. It is true that people respond to conflict and tough situations in different ways, and some people are more sensitive than others, but everyone deserves to work in a respectful environment. If a situation makes a person feel slighted, belittled, or angry, it is important to take an objective look at it

---

[65] Ibid

in order to determine whether they need to adjust themselves, or address it with someone.

Demanding Respect in the Workplace

How can a person demand respect in the workplace? Demand is a strong word. For that reason there has to be an art to it and a logical way to go about it. When it comes to demanding respect, does it mean that a person should walk around their workplace holding reports hostage, and throwing temper tantrums until they get what they want? Does demanding respect mean a person should bully and belittle others to incite fear with their presence? No, of course not. Demanding respect does not mean we purposefully cause problems or become a bully. A person should never have to be disrespectful to others in order to demand respect. Demanding respect does mean however, to take a stance and an active part in getting the respect they deserve and desire. Demanding respect in the workplace is in the way someone feels about themselves first and foremost. In order to demand respect, a person must know how to respect themselves when they are amongst others. If they do not have an adequate amount of self-respect, the demand for respect will come off as being unauthentic.

One of the ways women can demand respect in the workplace is through our communication style. Male and female communication styles can never be totally generalized, but there does tend to be some differences with how they communicate, and how they deliver a message. These differences also translate into the workplace. Women tend to use more indirect language and use more words when they speak to someone. They want to be understood, and so they are very detailed when they explain things, and the conversation can have many layers. Men tend to use more direct language in word choice, and use less words when they speak. Their conversation is more direct and straightforward. They get to the point faster. Neither is better than the other, however, in the workplace, women should be mindful of their speaking style and speak directly in order to demand respect from others. They should avoid using words that suggest someone do something, and use words that direct someone to do something instead. Examples of words and phrases used in direct communication are: "we should", "we will", "I'm sure that", "I'm confident that", "we need to", "we must", etc. Examples of words and phrases used in indirect communication are "I hope", "I feel", "I wish", "I was thinking", "would it be okay if", "maybe", etc.

Women also should appear confident and not arrogant in the workplace. Confident women in the workplace motivate and encourage others. Confidence shows that a woman knows she is great at what she does. Arrogance does the opposite, and makes a person look like the office jerk. Arrogant women in the workplace discourage others, tear them down, and come off as narcissistic or know-it-alls. This person is condescending and acts untouchable, as if they could never lose their job and it has a negative effect on their co-workers.

Another way to demand respect is to be assertive rather than aggressive in the workplace. Assertive people are able to communicate their ideas and opinions confidently and directly, and at the same time still respect others. Aggressive people need to control others, get their way, or intimidate others to feel respected. This is not truly respect, and it pushes others away from you and makes them resentful. This is not conducive to being someone who wants to be an assertive driving force in their workplace. In order to do so, the people around you have to look at you as a leader, no someone who will undermine them in order to get ahead.

When demanding respect in the workplace it is important for a woman to know her job. She should know the ins and outs of what she does, and exactly why it is important to the organization. Whatever she has noted as a strength during an interview process or an important project, should be a definite strength. Some people over sale themselves in an attempt to look good, and then cannot make good on the skills they are supposed to possess. When it is time to deliver at work, do not be the person who drops the ball. When a person is unprepared and has no choice except to allow someone else do the work they are supposed to be able to do, they will quickly lose respect.

Lastly women should use their emotional quotient skills in order to demand respect in the workplace. Emotional quotient (EQ) measures our emotional intelligence. In the article, "Emotional Intelligence", leading emotional intelligence researchers Peter Salovey and John D. Mayer, defined emotional intelligence, "as the subset of social intelligence that involves the ability to monitor one's own and others' feelings and emotions, discriminate among them and to use this information to guide one's thinking and actions."[66] Research has found that women generally have a higher EQ than men. Women are better at reading body language, detecting emotion in others, and women are more nurturing than men naturally. Although men do not do as well as women in those areas, they do tend to be better with keeping their emotions from affecting other areas of their lives. Still this means that women can approach business dealings from a more intuitive place. This is definitely something to be used to a woman's advantage. This does not mean that women should tip toe around the men they work with or be submissive to them. This advantage does mean that women should be able to use their EQ to navigate complex situations and conflict in a way that helps us to remain respectful while we demand the same.

Earning Respect in the Workplace

If demanding respect is related to respecting yourself and your level of self-worth in the workplace, then earning respect can be said to be related to how you respect others. Also, when a woman has earned respect in the workplace, she has made an investment in her company, and has become an asset to her team. Investments take time and hard work, and earning respect is proof of a woman's leadership skills at

---

[66] Salovey, P., Mayer, J. D. (1990). *Emotional Intelligence*. Imagination, Cognition and Personality. Baywood Publishing Co., Inc.

work. Respect is earned through having a healthy balance between speaking up for yourself and respecting others. A woman does not earn respect by being the workplace doormat. When a woman is too nice at work she may find herself having a hard time saying no. She may feel under-appreciated or have her kindness taken for granted. She may get stuck doing tasks that others do not want to do. She may also consistently take care of herself last and others first.

There are a number of ways a woman can earn respect in the workplace. These include being mindful of your professional appearance, doing great work, meeting deadlines, being a problem solver, being approachable, being considerate and patient, and attacking problems instead of attacking people. The woman who wants to earn respect in the workplace looks good at work. She dresses in a professional manner, and wears properly fitting clothes. She may dress casually or wear more corporate attire, but no matter what, she is always neat and put together.

This woman also does great work. When someone benefits the team, everyone knows that they are skilled at their job. Just as co-workers know exactly who the weak links of the team are, and who does not pull their weight at work, co-workers can recognize the stand out rock stars at work as well. This woman also meets work deadlines. A reliable reputation is a great way to earn respect. She is also approachable. She smiles and looks relaxed and comfortable. Sometimes certain facial expressions, dress style, or demeanor can make a person look mean or intimidating. This woman is mindful of this and takes steps to avoid giving that impression. Lastly, the woman who wants to earn respect is considerate and patient. She also **attacks problems instead of attacking people.** Wherever there are groups of people, there will eventually be conflict. A person can never control the other party, but they can control themselves. When problems do arise, the woman who earns respect is able to detach herself emotionally, and take the time to work towards a mutually beneficial solution. These are also all ways that women in the workplace can respect others. When women in the workplace treat others with respect with how they handle their work, and how they handle their work relationships, they make a lasting impression on their peers. People never forget how you make them feel.

Benefits of Being Respected in the Workplace

Respect is again, a basic human need. Everyone deserves respect, but in the workplace, it is not always simply given. Work is a large part of the activity that takes place during the human lifespan. About one-third of our lives are spent working.[67] This equates to about 90,000 hours spent working, according to Business Insider.[68] What a large chunk of time to be unhappy! This is why job satisfaction is so important, and a person cannot be satisfied if they do not feel respected. When women work hard to demand and earn respect, then they should reap the benefits of that hard work and feel respected at work. So what are these benefits? Being respected allows you to have more influence in the workplace. You become a more effective leader. People will ask for your opinion, and for input with decisions because your opinion will carry weight. You will have more confidence at work. This allows you to feel able to communicate and express your ideas freely, and to be taken seriously. Being able to do this helps you to have better relationships with your co-workers, and makes it easier to deal with a tough boss or a workplace bully. Lastly, it positions you to be an obvious choice for promotion opportunities and better pay. These benefits all play a part in the equation for job satisfaction. When you are able to be happy with your job and experience satisfaction at work on all of these levels, you become truly successful.

---

[67] What percentage of our lives are spent working? (n.d.). Retrieved on May 17, 2015 from http://www.ask.com/math/percentage-lives-spent-working-599e3f7fb2c88fca

[68] Shontell, A. (2011).15 Seriously Disturbing Facts About Your Job. Business Insider. Business Insider, Inc.

Summary

With so much of our lives spent in the workplace, women deserve to be respected, and deserve to have an enjoyable, bearable environment. The current statistics on where women stand in the workplace are known, and overall the future outlook on where women stand in the workplace look very promising. Still, it is necessary to take an active stance at work when it comes to earning and demanding respect, since it is not always given. First, women need to know if they are being disrespected. Then they need to adjust themselves in order to demand and earn respect, understanding that they do not have to disrespect or bully others, and that the goal is to be a valuable team member with great peer relationships. And lastly, they should focus on working for the respect that they deserve and enjoy the benefits that come with it. Women are strong, determined, and have the IQ and EQ necessary to continue to push forward and blaze trails. The future of the business world is in our hands, just step up, grab it and lead, in the way that only women can.

Chapter 4

Work/Life Balance

By: Aisha Martin
The Madness Maven
CEO and Sr. Advisor of A. Martin Group, LLC.
Founder of Precious Gems Worldwide
Serial Entrepreneur, United Nations Ambassador
Speaker, Author, Investor, PR and Business Professional,
Work/Life Balance Strategist, Co-Radio Host

The Tango

The idea of having a balanced life both in the home as well as out of the home is being challenged more and more. Time has proven, yet again, that things do indeed change. Societal norms of the time have shifted from prohibiting the employment of married women to women sitting on boards of million dollar companies and becoming successful entrepreneurs. With changes as drastic as these, women have become forced to make life decisions early: To get married or not? To have kids or not? To start a business or not? To climb the corporate ladder or simply settle? To go back to school? Write a book? Take that dream vacation or not? How is it possible to balance having a spouse, kids, becoming an entrepreneur (or serial), and/or work towards that promotion? A better question would be; "Can this be done with minimal stress and not getting overwhelmed?" It is time to consider that fact that having it all is quite possible.

Many researchers believe work-life balance is a myth that many want to believe is possible...like a stork delivering a baby instead of the grueling, intense pain of childbirth. Work-life balance is not just a coined phrase that sounds nice. However, there are levels to creating a balance that works to fit each individual. It is much like the term success. What success means to one person could differ greatly to the next person. Neither is right or wrong, just different. What balance means to one person could mean something completely different to another. Once the foundation is mastered, one can start the process of having and managing it all.

Foundation: The Non-negotiables

Non-negotiables are factors that a person will absolutely NOT compromise on. These will vary from person to person, and again, there is no right or wrong answer. Think of the classic family game, Jenga. It is the game where rectangular blocks are stacked across each other into a tall tower. Once the tower is built, each player takes a turn to strategically remove a block from the structure and place it back on top of the tower. It is easy in the beginning because the tower is solid, but over time, the structure has holes and gaps in it from the missing pieces. The player to stack as many blocks on top during their turn, without causing the tower to fall, is the winner. As women, we tend to always have on the "Superwoman" cape, the who woman handles, fixes, negotiates, finds and takes care of pretty much anything she touches. Plus, she does so while making it look extremely easy. What a gift! The problem is, if her foundation is not solid, holes and gaps, causing everything to fall, as with the Jenga game. Taking things as they come can lead to stress and other health issues when trying to manage so many responsibilities. Apart from responsibilities women have, it is good to have at least three non-negotiables to start her foundation. So how does one determine what is most important to them? This may take a little reflection time. Think about some of the following questions:

1. If I compromise this, will I have regrets or resentment?

2. Does this compromise my health?

3. Will I be able to sleep at night with a clear conscience?

4. Does this compromise my morals, values or spiritual beliefs?

If a woman has a family or spouse, one of her non-negotiables may be to be home to tuck her kids in at least three times a week. If she does not have children, but has a significant other, she may decide not to compromise their bi-weekly date night. Some other examples can be making time for meditation every morning, exercising at least four times a week, having a monthly girl's night, or shutting down all work by 10pm. These are all personal non-negotiables, but for work it translates the same way. The non-negotiables could be to take an extra training class once a month, to scout for at least two new clients per week, or to come in early once a week to have breakfast with management. Decide what is important and stick to it. The structure created will determine how well a person is able to manage balancing both life and work.

Scheduling: The System

Once the non-negotiables have been determined, it is vital to get a system in place that works for you. Scheduling helps to keep not only personal things organized, but work and business as well. Scheduling and planning not only helps a person to maximize their time, but it also helps to decrease stress. There are different opinions on the effectiveness of multitasking and whether doing so causes a person to not be as efficient in the tasks they are doing. It is easy to hear quotes like, "We all have the same 24 hours in a day as Oprah or Ivanka Trump" and feel something is wrong if a person does not accomplish what these women seem to claim in a day. There is one key factor that makes Oprah and Ivanka's 24 hours in a day different than many others. That factor is resources. While they have 24 hours just as anyone else, they also have the financial resources that allow them to delegate more than the average. The assistants, nannies, personal chefs, drivers, etc. that they have access to allows them to maximize their time so that they have multiple people assisting them achieve their goals. When one does not have access to these resources, one must find a way to get the most out of each and every single day.

The first thing to look at is common time wasters. These are things that call kill productivity and aid procrastination. Some of the most popular ones are:

1.   **Social Media** - People can spend countless hours on social media sites like Facebook, Twitter, Pinterest, Tumblr and Instagram. According to the 2012 *Nielsen's* annual Social Media report, the United States spent 121 billion minutes on social media in July 2012.[69]

2.   **Emails** - Technology is a great tool. However, with having immediate access to every email that comes in, it can become a big distraction. Try to only check your emails three times a day. Morning, afternoon, and evening if possible. If you are in the workplace, prioritize your emails. If possible, turn off phone notifications and pause your emails from constantly coming through. Services like Inboxpause.com allow you to check emails on your time instead of when the sender sends them. There is a difference between important and urgent.

3.   **Browsing the Internet** - Many are guilty of this. It is so easy to open a new tab when a quick idea pops up or click on an ad that is blinking on the screen. If an amazing idea just so happens to pop up (this tends to happen frequently with creatives), have a notepad or an app to document the idea for later on. Stay focused on what is currently at hand.

4.   **Watching Television** - Of course there is nothing wrong with watching television, but one must be mindful of how much. When it is time for work, work! There is no need to see what was missed on television. Ten minutes can easily turn into thirty minutes without second thought.

---

[69] Popkin, H. A.S. (2012).We Spent 230,060 Years on Social Media in One Month. CNBC.com. Retrieved April 25, 2015 from: http://www.cnbc.com/id/100275798

5.   **Phone calls** - Every phone call does not have to be answered at that particular moment. Remember the importance of prioritizing. Voicemail was created for a reason. Making the most out of the time allotted daily for calls will require sacrifices. When a moment presents itself, check for missed messages and respond accordingly.

6.   **Unnecessary Meetings** - When in the workplace, if the meeting is not mandatory, pause and take a minute to see how this meeting will be beneficial. If it will go over the company's new Standard Operating Procedure (SOP), that is understandable. If it will cover basic information already known, think twice about automatically going.

7.   **Online Games** - According to Forbes.com, online gaming is predicted to bring in $82 million by 2017.[70] Again, this can be a huge distraction when it is time to get work done. Prioritize and put this in your leisure time.

8.   **Indecisiveness** - Not being clear on what work-life balance choices to make, leads to more procrastination. Then this leads to not choosing anything, thus wasting time. If creating a pros/cons list, which includes writing all the pros and cons of a particular subject, and then making a decision, does not work, scheduling a time to thoroughly think things through may be needed.

Now that time wasters are out of the way, it is time to get to scheduling and planning. Scheduling helps a person to become more proactive than reactive, thus lowering high stress situations. How a person schedules and what they schedule is completely up to them. Examine the following examples:

---

[70] Gaudiosi, J. (2012). New Reports Forecast Global Video Game Industry Will Reach $82 Billion By 2017. Retrieved May 4, 2015, from http://www.forbes.com/sites/johngaudiosi/2012/07/18/new-reports-forecasts-global-video-game-industry-will-reach-82-billion-by-2017

Example 1:

Miranda has two businesses. One is a bakery and the other is an event planning business. She is single without children and recently went back to school to attain her Master's.

	Mon.	Tues.	Wed.	Thurs.	Fri.	Sat.
Morning	Bakery	Event	Bakery	Event	Bakery	Event
Afternoon	Exercise	School	Bakery	Exercise	Event	Bakery
Evening	School	School	Exercise	School	Event	Exercise

Miranda schedules out her priorities by morning, afternoon and evening at her leisure. This organizes when she does her school assignments, workout, and balance both businesses successfully. Sunday is not listed because it is her free day.

Example 2:

Lisa works a corporate job Monday through Friday. She is in the process of learning a new program that she has to study on her own time. Lisa is married with two teenagers and is also starting her own accounting firm.

	Monday	**Tuesday**	**Wednesday**	**Thursday**	**Friday**
6am	Workout	Business	Workout	Business	Workout
am-4pm	Work	Work	Work	Work	Work
7pm	Dinner and Family Time	Dinner and Family Time	Dinner and Family Time	Dinner and Family Time	Dinner and Family Time
pm-10pm	Reading	Business	Reading	Business	Go Out

For this schedule, Lisa is a bit more specific with time windows. She makes sure she has dedicated time to spend with her family (non-negotiable), gets in some "me" time with working out, has time for a weekly date night or social time, works on her future accounting business, and makes time to read up on the new program at her job.

Life happens and things do not always go according to plan. Having a schedule allows a person to see where they left off and makes it easier to regroup and continue to move forward. Also, have a cut off point for each day. By doing so, it prevents the feeling of having days running into each other. When managing multiple priorities, keep in mind to delegate what can be delegated, determine the level of importance and stick to your non-negotiables.

Priorities: Urgent Versus Important

It is important to be able to categorize situations as they happen. If not, a person could be easily overwhelmed. One way to categorize is to determine whether the task at hand is important or urgent. Sometimes people can use those two words interchangeably, but their meaning is completely different. According to Oxfordictionaries.com, the definition of urgent is: **Immediate action or attention**

Urgent matters are normally driven by external factors, such as deadlines. If a manager gives her employee a deadline for a key report, it is considered an urgent matter. If the fire alarm goes off in a building, people will rush out because their safety is an urgent matter. When it is time to go vote for officials, a person has to be at the polls by a certain time. That is considered to be urgent.

Oxforddictionaries.com defines important as: **Of great significance or value.** Important matters are normally driven by internal factors and vary from person to person. What may be important to one person may not necessarily be important to the next. Making time to work out three times per week can be important to Person A, but Person B hates the thought of working out. Getting advanced training on Excel formulas can be important to Person B, but not to Person A. Again, an important matter may not be urgent.

If a phone call is coming through and a person is in work mode, they should determine if that phone call is important or urgent. It is the same with emails. If the email is urgent, do what needs to be done to get it taken care of. If it is simply important, try your best to handle it by the end of the day, if possible.

Learn to Unplug

In a society full of "instant gratification", it is important to make time to unplug from it all. This allows time to recharge, reconnect and rejuvenate. The biggest hurdle many people have to learn is to unplug from their cellphones.

Research states:

> 67% of cell owners find themselves checking their phone for messages, alerts, or calls — even when they don't notice their phone ringing or vibrating. Some 18% of cell owners say that they do this "frequently."
>
> 44% of cell owners have slept with their phone next to their bed because they wanted to make sure they didn't miss any calls, text messages, or other updates during the night.
>
> 29% of cell owners describe their cell phone as "something they can't imagine living without."
>
> 24% of cell owners say that the worst thing about cell ownership is that they are constantly available and can be reached at any time. [71]

Because of statistics like these, it would be easiest to take baby steps with unplugging. Remember, for success with work-life balance, the idea is to have a solid foundation, like Jenga. Start by placing cell phones and tablets in another room at night. It is not as easy to check them when they are not within a hand's distance.

---

[71] Smith, A. (2012) The Best (and Worst) of Mobile Connectivity. Retrieved May 4, 2015, from http://www.pewinternet.org/2012/11/30/the-best-and-worst-of-mobile-connectivity

Once the night time anxiety is no longer an issue, try some time during the day. If at the workplace, try muting devices and placing them in a drawer near you. The idea is to get the devices off of the physical body (pockets, purse, etc.) and out of sight, out of mind for 10 minute intervals. Once the initial 10 minutes are no longer an issue, try to extend the time to 20 minutes and continue to increase the intervals. If a person is not in the workplace, it will be easier to schedule a "break" from their devices. Schedule a time to cut off phones and tablets. Also during this time, step AWAY from the computer. Go read a book, meditate, take a walk, take a nap, anything else that does not involve being "plugged in" to work. This allows creativity to flow and helps with de-stressing.

Me Time: A Must Have

"Me time" was discussed briefly in the "Learn to Unplug" section, but it is time for a more in depth look. "Me time" is just that....personal time to get back to you. Women are natural nurturers and can easily become caught up in the needs of others. If women are constantly giving mentally, emotionally, spiritually and physically to others, but are not replenishing themselves while doing so, they will not be able to give for long. "Me time" is a non-negotiable for many, as it should be. If scheduled correctly, it can be a daily treat. Here are some ways to have "me time".

1.Reading a book - Reading helps release creative energy and frees the imagination.

2.Take deep breaths - Relax and become centered with controlled breaths.

3.Listen to music

4.Chat with a good friend

5.Get a massage/manicure/pedicure

6. Go see a movie or play

7. Complete a crossword puzzle

8. Plan a trip or something exciting to look forward to outside of work duties.

9. Take a nap

10. Bubble bath

11. Take a class or try something completely new.

12. Drink a cup of tea or coffee and just be in the moment

"Me time" should be scheduled a couple of times per day, even if it is two 15-minutes sessions. If scheduling daily seems a bit overwhelming initially, try scheduling weekly. Keep in mind, "me time" is about letting go of stress, so there should be excitement when scheduling it. It is something to look forward to, remember?

Technology: The Good Side

As much as technology has created a society that finds it hard to disconnect, technology can be used to help manage work and life. From applications to alarms, there are now personal assistants within an arm's reach. The convenience to be able to connect at any given time can be a great thing. Services such as online bill pay, online banking and online shopping have changed how many businesses connect with their customers.

> When it comes to the positive effects, the difference between millennials and non-millennials differ:
>
> 85% of millennials said they are excited to try new technology, compared to 64% of non-millennials.

84% of millennials said they are able to do more in less time with their technology, compared to 68% of non-millennials.

52% of millennials said they have more time for family and friends because technology enables them to do work from anywhere, compared to 42% of non-millennials.[72]

When looking at a survey of internet users between the ages of 13 to 91:

74% of respondents said they are able to do more in less time with their technology.

72% are excited to try new technology.

45% said they would rather work remotely than in the office.

45% said they have more time for their family and friends because technology enables them to do work from anywhere. 25% reported that they struggle to figure out new technology.[73]

So how can technology help with the work-life balance tango? Not everyone has a notebook and pen handy. Use applications like Evernote or the voice recorder to document those fleeting ideas and reminders that come up. For example, if Lisa (our example person from earlier) is catching up on reading or at work and an idea about her accounting business comes up, she can record the thought and return to it later when she has the time. This helps to eliminate distractions and improve productivity. Lisa would be able to stay focused on the task at hand instead of trying to multi-task. Everything has a time, place and space. Once those three are determined, it makes it easier to balance wearing multiple hats. Another example of how technology can

---

[72] The benefits - and drawbacks - of online technology. (2013). USC. Retrieved May 4, 2015, from http://news.usc.edu/54256/the-benefits-and-drawbacks-of-online-technology
[73] Ibid

help with the work-life balance tango is by saving time. Online banking and bill paying were mentioned earlier, but technology can also be great for setting reminders. Utilize the calendars in cell phones. If there is an important meeting at work that a woman has to prepare for, she can put it in their calendar and set a reminder for a day or two prior for preparation. Lastly, take advantage of the convenience that technology brings Have groceries or a pizza delivered for that girl's night in. Connect with the local taxi service or schedule your hair appointments with the touch of a finger. This will free up even more time.

The Pursuit of Perfection

As much as a living in a perfect world sounds ideal, it is not the reality. There is nothing wrong with wanting things to be perfect, but one has to be able to accept their best. Work and life balance will not, and cannot be, achieved if the end goal is perfection. A woman has to know that their best is good enough. It is not settling or slacking. It is **THEIR** version of perfection. How a woman feels will dictate their actions. It is okay for a woman to give herself permission to be okay with achieving what she can, when she can, without the outside stereotypes and criticism. For example, if a woman is used to having laundry washed, folded and put up all in one day and that suddenly changes, it is okay. Because of her schedule, non-negotiables or simply life happening, that task may change to being done a Thursday, the clothes being left in a dryer for a day or so, being folded on Saturday and being away on Sunday. Another example is a group project due for work or school. Everyone is aware of the deadline, yet one person is so set on the goal of perfection that they put off completing their part until the last minute. This forces them to rush and cram, when that could have been avoided from the beginning. The reality of that situation is this: their idea of perfection is now farther away because of procrastination, and because they chose to let fear and anxiety prevent them from starting. Schedules change and a person has to be able to adapt to change when needed.

Perfectionism can also lead to procrastination and high anxiety. If a person dreads the thought of a poor performance, they will feel the anxiety from the fear they are experiencing. So how does a person know if they suffer from this perfectionism-procrastination process?

1.　They hold to lofty standards.

2.　They have no guarantee they will do well enough.

3.　Less than the best is not an option.

4.　As they think of not doing well enough, they feel uncomfortable.

5.　They fear the feelings of discomfort.

6.　They hide their imperfections from themselves and dodge discomfort by doing something "safer," such as playing computer games.

7.　They repeat this exhausting process until they get off their contingent-worth merry-go-round by working to do better while not demanding perfection from themselves.[74]

Environment: Being Selfish

This is one of the most important keys to having a successful work-life balance. Be selfish. Yes, selfish. Being selfish has been made into a somewhat negative villainous trait. A woman must understand that it is important to "pay" herself first, that includes financially, emotionally, physically and spiritually. Of course, there is absolutely nothing wrong with giving to charities or whatever cause a woman deems worthy of her time and/or money. One area a woman has to evaluate even closer is her own environment; including family, friends, associates,

---

[74] Knaus, B. (2010). Break a Perfectionism-Procrastination Connection. Retrieved May 4, 2015, from https://www.psychologytoday.com/blog/science-and-sensibility/201003/break-perfectionism-procrastination-connection

coworkers, colleagues, and other close relationships. Empty conversations, poorly planned meetings, and activities that do not add value to a woman's well-being should be thought out making a commitment. Children can have, in their opinion, an urgent matter because they cannot find a particular shirt, for example. That is not urgent, that is important to them. A colleague may want to gossip about the latest news around the water cooler, but that does not add value. Being able to decide who, what, when, and how a woman interacts with others, helps her to stay in control of her atmosphere.

Summary

The goal to having it all and having a successful work-life balance is to discover what works for each individual. A woman may be able to handle more than the next, and there is nothing wrong with that. Do not compare plates or measure whose grass is greener. The greener the grass, the more it has to be watered!

Chapter 5

"Standitioning" from the Workplace to Entrepreneurship

By: LaKisha C Brooks and Sabrina Brawner

Why Do Women "Standition" from the Workplace to Entrepreneurship?

In Chapter 1, we learned that women are grossly underrepresented in leadership and decision making positions in the United States. Additionally, women experience salary inequality, are facing challenges balancing work and life, and, at times, are discriminated against or disrespected in the workplace. Women are becoming frustrated, are demanding answers and actions, and they are beginning to seek other options. If women continue to endure these issues in the workplace, more and more will decide to make a "standition". A standition is a period in time when someone is ready to take a stand on what he or she believes in order to transition to the next phase of his or her life. In this case, a standition for a frustrated woman may include becoming an entrepreneur. When the standition takes place, women use their talents, skills and experience to create their own rules and path to a successful business. This chapter will provide women with tips and tools needed to "standition" from the workplace to entrepreneurship.

The Pros and Cons of Starting Your Own Business

Being an entrepreneur is one of the most rewarding ways for someone to express their passions and interests, and being "your own boss" can be a thrilling concept. Some people may envision an exciting lifestyle for themselves as an entrepreneur, full of fun, travel, and glamour, or a fulfilling and comfortable retirement. Others may just dislike their job, or want to seek a better income. No matter what reasons a woman has for wanting to start a business, she should definitely understand exactly what she is getting themselves into, by learning all she can about their potential business, and by mapping out the pros and cons.

There are many "pros," to owning a business, as well as many possible "cons." Depending on the industry a woman may want to enter, her current job or lifestyle, or her personality, she may view the advantages, and disadvantages, or challenges to owning a business differently than others. This means that when figuring out pros and cons, a woman will need to be as specific as possible by factoring in her own values and personal goals. Below is a list of general guidelines that can be used when detailing these comparisons.

Pros

1. The ability to be your own boss, and the career security that comes with it. You don't have to worry about getting fired, or wait years and years for a promotion dependent on seniority.

2. The ability to set your own working hours.

3. No ceiling or a more flexible ceiling on your income than you would obtain through a salaried position as an employee.

4. The joy of being passionate about your work.

5. The ability to use your own creativity to bring your own vision to life.

6. The freedom to work from home, or your favorite coffee shop, or the beach—wherever you like.

7. The ability to grow and learn professionally at an accelerated rate through hands on business experience.

8. The ability to have more control to balance your work life and your personal life.

9. The ability to help others by providing employment opportunities, while at the same time growing your business.

10. The excitement of working for yourself. Every day is different, and there are no dull moments as a business owner.

Cons

1. You have to be extremely self-motivated. As your own boss, there is no one there pushing you to get your work done, and there is no paid sick leave or vacation time.

2. Although you can set your own working hours, it is common for new business owners to work long hours, and on weekends, while they are getting their business of the ground.

3. Starting a new business will undoubtedly require that you make sacrifices in your personal life in the beginning, because of limited time. This can cause a strain in your relationships with family or friends.

4. You will have to invest money before you can make a return, and a return is not guaranteed.

5. The buck stops with you. Every decision and step is in your hands, along with the consequences, if you make or take the wrong ones. This type of responsibility can be overwhelming and stressful.

6. You could fail. Many small businesses that start off with a great idea and vision, never make it off the ground, due to foundational problems or lack of funds.

7. It's not as glamourous as it seems. Yes, you will be a business owner, but you may also need to be a secretary, repair person, manager, or at times a janitor.

8. If you hire employees, managing them can be challenging. You have to depend on them for your business to go smoothly, while not

being able to predict what will happen in their personal lives, or how they will perform on a daily basis. You also have to be willing to hire and fire them.

9. Never knowing what to expect. Every day will be different, and some excitement comes with that. However, it can also bring stress. You may have to frequently start your day with a problem that needs solving. If a product or tool breaks down, you will have to fix it or replace it ASAP in order for business to continue to run smoothly.

Women interested in taking the step towards becoming a business owner must empower themselves to make the decision, by ensuring that they are thoroughly educated, have defined goals, and are driven enough to finish the course. The Small Business Administration, or SBA, lists the following questions to consider when determining what your strengths and weaknesses are when it comes to owning a business:

- Are you a self-starter?
- How well do you handle different personalities?
- How good are you at making decisions?
- Do you have enough physical and emotional stamina?
- How well do you plan and organize?
- Is your drive strong enough to maintain your motivation?
- How will owning a business affect your family?[75]

Considering these questions can help women to visualize what their lives as a business owner will look like, so that they can determine if they are ready. If they are not ready, this may just mean that more preparation is needed. There are always classes, and trainings that women can take in order to develop areas of weakness so that they become strengths. The SBA also provides an assessment at

---

[75] Small Business Administration. (n.d.). Retrieved August 25, 2015, from https://www.sba.gov/sites/default/files/files/resourceguide_3157.pdf

www.sba.gov/assessmenttool/index.html[76], in order to provide further help with figuring out if you are ready.

How to Be a Part Time Entrepreneur

One of the most empowering things about becoming a business owner is the ability to be in control. Business owners control their time, the decision making, and the details of the business. Depending on the structure of the business, there still may be guidelines, or rules that have to be followed, possibly with a partnership, a franchise business, or the purchase of a pre-existing business. Still, the business owner runs most of the show, if not all. Some women decide to leave the workplace altogether to start a business, taking a leap of faith, and hoping that they are a success. This is a fine idea, if a woman has income to use in order to support herself if it does not work out, or if she has the ability to go back to a guaranteed job. Many women do not have this luxury and instead, may decide to stay in the workplace, while building their business at the same time. Some may never want to leave the workplace, while others may be waiting for their business to take off, so they can leave when desired. For those women who are "standitioning" from the workplace into entrepreneurship, success is definitely obtainable, despite the sometimes seemingly overwhelming number of tasks, and details that it takes to get a business off the ground, and to thrive. It takes discipline, but there are a number of things women can do to get the most out of being a part-time entrepreneur:

1.   **Keep Your Job and Your Business Separate**. It is important to make sure you are not working on your own business on company time and equipment. You also want to make sure that you are legally able to pursue your business. Do not violate a non-compete agreement and risk getting fired or sued.

---

[76] Ibid

2.   **Make Time**. You will need to schedule time to work on your business. You may decide to take an hour a day, or a few hours every other day. Schedule it out, and stick to it as closely as possible. You may need to utilize both nights and weekends, if you have a full time job.

3.   **Reduce Distractions**. You may need to sacrifice television and phone time. You may decide to turn off all devices during your entrepreneurship time. You will need to be able to focus.

4.   **Set Goals**. You should have weekly or monthly SMART (Specific, Measurable, Attainable, Realistic & Relevant, and Time Based) Goals, and you should focus on them one at a time instead of multi-tasking. You should also set long term goals.

5.   **Share the Work.** If you can afford help, get it, in the form of accounting software such as QuickBooks, a website designer, or an assistant. You can also barter services with people/companies instead. Another possibility would be to get help from friends or family.

6.   **Be Strategic With Time.** Entrepreneurship is a lifestyle. You should always socialize with a purpose. When you get some leisure time, you may benefit from participating in entrepreneurship trainings, or networking opportunities, instead of doing random activities or "hanging out."

7.   **Utilize Social Media**. Open up free accounts with all of the relevant social media companies such as Facebook, LinkedIn, Instagram, Twitter, and Google+. This gets your name out there, and makes your business searchable. Also put your business information in the signature lines of your personal email, and direct people to your website or contact information there.

8. **Promote Daily**. Find ways to let people know you are in business with or without physically telling them. There are certain places we visit frequently or daily. Ask if there is an area to post your business flyer or business card there. Put a bumper sticker or a magnet on your car, or get a window cling made to place on your car.

9. **Get Feedback From Family, Friends, and Clients**. Ask for feedback on marketing or branding materials or reviews on your services.

10. **Take time For Yourself**. You will get mentally and physically tired. Make sure you are setting aside time to "do nothing." Relax alone, or with family and recharge.

Use Your Current Role to Learn How to be an Entrepreneur

Perhaps a woman is considering making a standition, and she has a full time job and is not quite ready to become an entrepreneur; what should she do? She should use her current position as a planting moment to sow her seeds while she is preparing for entrepreneurship. When working for any company, a woman should see her job as a business within a business. Yes, she is working for a company and working to meet her goals and expectations, but she also goes to work for herself, striving to accomplish her own goals within the company. Her boss assigns her tasks to complete, clients to work with, and ideas to formulate. "She has her own book of business". This means she will always have her own tasks to accomplish for the company. Not only will these tasks help her gain tangible skills, but she can also gain intangible skills while on the job. These skills include conflict management, teamwork, problem solving and decision making; talents needed for entrepreneurship. She should show initiatives on her job, stand out, be a leader, and start having the entrepreneurial mindset. Having this mindset will be to her advantage when she becomes an entrepreneur. Also, she should take time to speak with and consult with upper management. Revealing a plan to standition may not be ideal, but a woman should pick the brains of her management team. Learn how leaders think, act, dress, and talk. These are free resources to help understand management and how a business is ran.

Have a Plan

This may be the most important step to standition into entrepreneurship. If the goal is to leave a current employer and become an entrepreneur, it will take a carefully thought out plan. It is not merely "I hate my job; and I don't like my boss. I want to quit and work for myself." A woman has to really determine if this is the right decision for her. Not only should she determine if this is the right decision, but consider if it is the right time. Timing is everything. Just because she wants to quit, it may not be the right time to quit. A woman may not be completely ready for the journey she is about to embark on. Determining that this is the best decision is only part of having a plan; S.M.A.R.T goals must also be set. Goals can be set by asking some of these questions. How long will I be with my current employer? How much capital do I need to get started? How will I get capital? Will I need an office space? Have I developed my business and marketing plan? Just because a woman wants to quit her job that does not mean her bills will stop accruing. She must have a plan in the event she does not acquire customers or clients right out the gate. The money she has saved may go towards all of her bills within months. She may then find herself inventing ways to generate more income. According to Forbes magazine, eight out of 10 businesses fail within the first 18 month[77]. If her business does fail, however, she should not see it as a negative, but view it as an opportunity of growth.

---

[77] Wagner. E.T. (2013). Five Reasons 8 Out Of 10 Businesses Fail. Forbes. Retrieved on May 17, 2015, from: http://www.forbes.com/sites/ericwagner/2013/09/12/five-reasons-8-out-of-10-businesses-fail/

Let Go of Fear

Being an entrepreneur and standitioning can be an exhilarating, yet scary process. A woman would be leaving behind a stable career and steady income to take the plunge into entrepreneurship. The fear of the unknown can stifle someone and be her worst enemy. The beauty of embarking on this journey is not knowing and trusting in one's abilities, experiences, and plan. Letting go of fear means allowing one to be vulnerable and fail. Failure is a possibility; however, it should not stop a woman from fulfilling her purpose and standitioning into entrepreneurship.

Passion and Purpose

Chapter 2 of *Leadership's Got Everything to Do With It*, talks about the importance of finding one's passion and discovering one's purpose.

Before embarking on the journey of working for herself, a woman must first know herself, know who she is and what she stands for. She must discover her passions and know her purpose. In order to do so, these questions should be answered.

1. What do I enjoy doing?
2. What are my motivations?
3. What are my strengths?
4. What is my ideal lifestyle?
5. What would I do if money was not a factor?
6. Why am I really standitioning?

Once a woman is able to answer these questions, she will then be able to take that stand because she knows and understands what she is supposed to be doing with her life. How does this translate into entrepreneurship? When she knows her purpose, a woman can begin to feel empowered; she will begin to gain confidence and begin to find a new career doing what she loves to do. She will no longer have to feel subjected to being overlooked for leadership and decision making positions, unequal wages for the same job as her male counterparts, or disrespect in the workplace.

Summary

With a lack of women in leadership and important decision making roles in the workplace, some are opting to take matters into their own hands and standition into entrepreneurship. The notion of being an entrepreneur is becoming a reality for many women as they continue to face issues such as unequal pay, disrespect in the workplace and no work-life balance. If a woman elects to make this journey, it is important to understand both the pros and cons of the decision, as entrepreneurship is not always the easiest mountain to climb. In addition to knowing the pros and cons, women should also have a well thought out plan to reduce the chances of failure. Most importantly, though failure is a possibility, women should let go of fear and just make the standition!

Conclusion

Women truly hold more power than we have ever been acknowledged and credited for. Collectively women are a force to be reckoned with. We continue to grow professionally in record numbers through education, and leadership positions; it is inevitable that we will change the face of the business world. As this transition takes place, women will undoubtedly bring with them fresh new perspectives that will replace traditional or dated ways of thinking, and doing business. Women have been brimming with great ideas, and ambitious desires, that for over 200 years have been blocked, held back, or limited because we did not have the means or power to express, and/or implement them. The female collective conscious remember this, and is aware that now we are privy to a level of freedom that has not been held for very long. Now unrestrained, women are ready and able to continue to innovate the workplace, and problem solve the issues that have limited us.

What Must be Done?

Those in current leadership positions must recognize the importance of cultivating female talent within their organizations so that women can advance in the workplace. Women have proven that they can "flat out lead." Organizations must assist women in this effort, and organizational leaders must utilize the four R's: Recruit, Refine, Recognize, and Retain. In turn, women must be willing to step up to the plate. If we are qualified and interested, we must not shy away from STEM (Science, Technology, Engineering, and Math) jobs. We must challenge the notion of what people view as "men jobs," and "women jobs." We have to seek out mentors and sponsors in our fields to help us. Lastly we have got to work effectively with each other.

Society as a whole has to recognize the economic implications for women, and their families when women are underpaid. With more women now heading households, it is imperative that women advance so that families can advance. To stunt the economic growth of women is to stunt the economic growth of the United States, and the world. Women must stand up for better pay when it is warranted, and refuse to settle for a portion of what men make for the same work. Women also must overcome these challenges by protecting themselves financially. We have got to take steps to become as financially literate as possible, budget properly, and invest aggressively.

Next, women have to demand and earn respect in the workplace through consistency, hard work, and dedication. As women we are already likely to be viewed differently than men in the workplace, and we are more likely to be judged more harshly when it comes to handling situations in the workplace. How we carry ourselves is very important, and it affects how we demand and earn respect. We must figure out how to demand respect while respecting others. We must learn the balance between confidence and arrogance—between aggressiveness and assertiveness. Women should also be aware of their professional appearance and their demeanor in order to earn respect. Through these steps we become an asset to our organization, in a position of value that brings us satisfaction.

Women also have to take care of themselves. We cannot advance in the workplace or within our businesses if we are burnt out. As women take on more responsibility, and juggle multiple aspects of their lives, they must not neglect themselves. Work-life balance is just that—balance. This does not mean that the scales will always be even, but by organizing our life activities, we are able to live the lives that make us happy, and still be productive. Be selfish sometimes. Take "me time," as needed. Women have to ensure that mental and physical health remains just as much a priority, as advancing at work.

Finally, women have to know when to take a stand. Women have been standitioning, throughout history. Women standition, when they decide it is time to start a business, and they standition, when they decide it is time to leave the workplace. When women are ready to become entrepreneurs, they should be clear on the pros and cons of business ownership. Preparation is a must when the expected outcome is success. Make smart decisions. If it is not time to leave the workplace, it's okay. Women can make part time entrepreneurship work for them.

From reviewing the history of women in business, we can see that women have not held the rights that closely affect us in the workplace for very long. It seems that the traditional attitude that says that women should not have to work, still follows us today. Tradition aside, the question has always been: What about the women who want to work? Women should not have been prevented from working because they were women, and they definitely should not have been prohibited from working in certain fields just because they were women. This very attitude, that has granted men more power and autonomy over women in the workplace to this day, is the one we must fight. So we have to continue to strive to enable those women who not only want to work, but who want to break down barriers and push past limitations imposed solely because of gender bias. Now that we know what must be done, it is time to take action. Challenge yourself and other women to **Learn, Lead, and Leave a Legacy in the Workplace** that is undeniable and unforgettable!

References

10 Surprising Statistics on Women in the Workplace | WorkplaceRantings.com. (n.d.). Retrieved on May 1, 2015 from: http://www.workplacerantings.com/10-surprising-statistics-on-women-in-the-workplace

15 Years Old and Over by Total Money Earnings in 2013, Age, Race, Hispanic Origin, and Sex, available at http://www.census.gov/hhes/www/cpstables/032014/perinc/toc.htm

Ackerman, H. (1964). "Bewitched". Los Angeles, CA: American Broadcasting Company

American Women in World War II. (n.d.). Retrieved August 24, 2015, from http://www.history.com/topics/world-war-ii/american-women-in-world-war-ii

Badal, S. B. (2014). The Business Benefits of Gender Diversity.Gallup. Retrieved on March 16, 2016 from: http://www.gallup.com/businessjournal/166220/business-benefits-gender-diversity.aspx

The benefits - and drawbacks - of online technology. (2013). USC. Retrieved May 4, 2015, from http://news.usc.edu/54256/the-benefits-and-drawbacks-of-online-technology

Brooks (2014) Leadership's Got Everything to Do With It: Women's Guide to the Sustainable Leader and Organization. Atlanta, GA. LaKisha C. Brooks

Connelly, J., Moshe, B. (1957). "Leave It Beaver". Los Angeles, CA: Columbia Broadcasting System and American Broadcasting Company

Coverture. (n.d.) West's Encyclopedia of American Law, edition 2. (2008). Retrieved August 23 2015 from http://legal-dictionary.thefreedictionary.com/coverture

Dawn. (n.d.) Single Mother Statistics. Single Mother Guide. Retrieved on May 3, 2015 from: https://singlemotherguide.com/

Discrimination by Type.Types of Discrimination. (n.d.) Retrieved on May 2, 2015 from http://eeoc.g Maslow's Hierarchy of Needs. (2007). Simply Psychology. Retrieved on April 27, 2015 from: http://www.simplypsychology.org/maslow.html

Dominici, F., Fried, L. P., & Zeger, S. L. (2009). So few women leaders. Academe

Facts About Life 2013. Retrieved May 10, 2015, from http://www.limra.com/uploadedFiles/limracom/Posts/PR/LIAM/PDF/Facts-Life-2013.pdf

Fairchild, C. (2015). The 23 Fortune 500 companies with all-male boards. Fortune Magazine. Retrieved on March 2, 2015 from: http://fortune.com/2015/01/16/fortune-500-companies-with-all-male-boards/

The Family and Medical Leave Act of 1993.(1993). Wage and Hour Division (WHD). United States Department of Labor

Friedan, B. (1963). Feminine Mystique. New York, NY

Gaudiosi, J. (2012). New Reports Forecast Global Video Game Industry Will Reach $82 Billion By 2017. Retrieved May 4, 2015, from http://www.forbes.com/sites/johngaudiosi/2012/07/18/new-reports-forecasts-global-video-game-industry-will-reach-82-billion-by-2017

A History of Women's Job. (n.d.). Retrieved August 24, 2015, from http://www.localhistories.org/womensjobs.html

Jacobe, D. (2013, June 3). One in Three Americans Prepare a Detailed Household Budget. Retrieved April 14th, 2015 from http://www.gallup.com/poll/162872/one-three-americans-prepare-detailed-household-budget.aspx

Kante, H. (1968). "Julia". Los Angeles, CA: American Broadcasting Company

Knaus, B. (2010). Break a Perfectionism-Procrastination Connection. Retrieved May 4, 2015, from https://www.psychologytoday.com/blog/science-and-sensibility/201003/break-perfectionism-procrastination-connection

Krawcheck, S. (2015). Why the Retirement Crisis is Also a Women's Crisis. Retrieved April 27, 2015, from http://www.washingtonpost.com/news/get-there/wp/2015/04/24/why-the-retirement-savings-crisis-is-also-a-womens-crisis/

Lewis, J. (n.d.). Women and Labor in Early America. Retrieved August 24, 2015, from http://womenshistory.about.com/od/worklaborunions/a/early_america.htm

Llopis, G. (2011). 4 Skills that Give Women a Sustainable Advantage Over Men. Forbes.com. Retrieved from: http://www.forbes.com/sites/glennllopis/2011/08/22/4-skills-that-give-women-a-sustainable-advantage-over-men/

Marksjarvis, G. (2015). Americans ill-prepared for retirement, survey finds. Retrieved April 13, 2015, from http://www.chicagotribune.com/business/yourmoney/ct-marksjarvis-0422-biz-20150421-column.html

Metro lyrics. It's a Man's Man's Man's World (New York: King Records, 1966), http://www.metrolyrics.com/its-a-mans-mans-world-lyrics-james-brown.html

Metrolyrics, Run the World (Girls) (New York: Columbia Records, 2011), http://www.metrolyrics.com/run-the-world-lyrics-beyonce.html

Meyers, L. (2013). Peek Inside the Book That Sparked a Second Wave of Feminism. Retrieved from: http://www.popsugar.com/love/Betty-Friedan-Feminine-Mystique-Quotes-28158627

Mulshine, M. (2015). Kevin O'Leary of 'Shark Tank' invests in 27 companies and says the only ones making money have female CEOs. Retrieved May 19, 2015, from http://www.businessinsider.com/kevin-olearys-female-ceos-make-all-the-money-2015-5

National Association of Women Business Owners. (n.d.). Retrieved on May 12, 2015 from: http://nawbo.org/section_103.cfm

Nelson, S. (2014). The Woman Code: 20 Powerful Keys to Unlock Your Life. Grand Rapids, MI. Baker Publishing Group

NWLC calculations from U.S. Census Bureau, Current Population Survey, 2014 Annual Social and Economic Supplement [hereinafter CPS, 2014 ASEC], Table PINC-05: Work Experience in 2013 – People O'Brien, S. A.(n.d.). 78 cents on the dollar: The facts about the gender wage gap. CNN Money. Retrieved from: http://money.cnn.com/2015/04/13/news/economy/equal-pay-day-2015/

Popkin, H. A.S. (2012).We Spent 230,060 Years on Social Media in One Month. CNBC.com. Retrieved April 25, 2015 from: http://www.cnbc.com/id/100275798

Ragsdale, C. (n.d.) Retrieved on May 12, 2015 from: http://www.whodoyourespect.com/withholding-respect-being-disrespected-clues/

Respect (n.d.). Retrieved on May 20, 2015 : from http://www.merriam-webster.com/dictionary/respect

Salmon, M. The Legal Status of Women, 1776–1830. (n.d.). Retrieved August 24, 2015, from http://www.gilderlehrman.org/history-by-era/womens-history/essays/legal-status-women-1776–1830

Sam Denoff, S., Persky, B., Thomas, M., Thomas, D. (1966). "That Girl". Los Angeles, CA: American Broadcasting Company

Salovey, P., Mayer, J. D. (1990). Emotional Intelligence. Imagination, Cognition and Personality. Baywood Publishing Co., Inc.

Shellenberger, S. (2012) The XX Factor: What's Holding Women Back? The Wall Street Journal. Retrieved on June 1, 2014 from: http://online.wsj.com/news/articles/SB10001424052702304746604577381953238775784

Shontell, A. (2011).15 Seriously Disturbing Facts About Your Job. Business Insider. Business Insider, Inc.

Single Mother Guide. (2015). Retrieved May 15, 2015, from https://singlemotherguide.com/single-mother-statistics/

Small Business Administration. (n.d.). Retrieved August 25, 2015, from https://www.sba.gov/sites/default/files/files/resourceguide_3157.pdf

Smith, A. (2012) The Best (and Worst) of Mobile Connectivity. Retrieved May 4, 2015, from http://www.pewinternet.org/2012/11/30/the-best-and-worst-of-mobile-connectivity

Storrie, M. (2012) The Business Imperative: Recruiting, Developing and Retaining Women in the Workplace. UNC Kenan-Flagler Business School. Retrieved on June 2, 2014 from: http://www.kenan-flagler.unc.edu/executive-development/custom-programs/~/media/3A15E5EC035F420690175C21F9048623.pdf

U.S. Census Bureau – Table C2. Household Relationship and Living Arrangements of Children Under 18 Years, by Age and Sex: 2014

U.S. Department of the Treasury, Internal Revenue Service, Topic 751. Washington, DC: 2015. Retrieved on May 7, 2015, from: http://www.irs.gov/taxtopics/tc751.html

Wagner. E.T. (2013). Five Reasons 8 Out Of 10 Businesses Fail. Forbes. Retrieved on May 17, 2015, from: http://www.forbes.com/sites/ericwagner/2013/09/12/five-reasons-8-out-of-10-businesses-fail/

The Wage Gap is Stagnant for Nearly a Decade. (2014). Retrieved May 12, 2015, from http://www.nwlc.org/resource/wage-gap-stagnant-nearly-decade

Walsh, K. (2010). The 1960s: A Decade of Change for Women. Retrieved April 17, 2015, from http://www.usnews.com/news/articles/2010/03/12/the-1960s-a-decade-of-change-for-women

What percentage of our lives are spent working? (n.d.). Retrieved on May 17, 2015 from http://www.ask.com/math/percentage-lives-spent-working-599e3f7fb2c88fca

When and how was NOW founded? (n.d.). Retrieved on March 22, 2015 from: http://now.org/faq/when-and-how-was-now-founded/

Wolf, W., & Fligstein, N. (1979). Sex and Authority in the Workplace: The Causes of sexual inequality. Retrieved April 13, 2015, from http://www.jstor.org/stable/2094507?seq=1#page_scan_tab_contents

Women CEOs of the S&P 500. (2015) Catalyst. Retrieved on April 6, 2015 from: http://www.catalyst.org/knowledge/women-ceos-sp-500

Women in the Labor Force. (n.d.). Retrieved August 24, 2015, from http://www.anb.org/cush_wlabor.html

Women in the Labor Force: A Databook. (2013).Retrieved May 12, 2015, from http://www.bls.gov/cps/wlf-databook-2012.pdf

Workplace Bullying Institute. (n.d.) Retrieved from on April 17, 2015: http://www.workplacebullying.org/ov/laws/types/index.cfm

Working and Voting -- Women in the 1920s. (n.d.). Retrieved August 24, 2015, from http://www.americanhistoryusa.com/working-voting-women-1920s/

www.ingramcontent.com/pod-product-compliance
Lightning Source LLC
Chambersburg PA
CBHW030914180526
45163CB00004B/1825